Cambridge Elements ≡

Elements in Quantitative and Computational Methods
for the Social Sciences
edited by
R. Michael Alvarez
California Institute of Technology
Nathaniel Beck
New York University

IMAGES AS DATA FOR SOCIAL SCIENCE RESEARCH

An Introduction to Convolutional Neural Nets for Image Classification

Nora Webb Williams
University of Illinois Urbana-Champaign
Andreu Casas
Vrije Universiteit Amsterdam
John D. Wilkerson
University of Washington

T0349750

CAMBRIDGE
UNIVERSITY PRESS

CAMBRIDGE
UNIVERSITY PRESS

University Printing House, Cambridge CB2 8BS, United Kingdom

One Liberty Plaza, 20th Floor, New York, NY 10006, USA

477 Williamstown Road, Port Melbourne, VIC 3207, Australia

314–321, 3rd Floor, Plot 3, Splendor Forum, Jasola District Centre,
New Delhi – 110025, India

79 Anson Road, #06–04/06, Singapore 079906

Cambridge University Press is part of the University of Cambridge.

It furthers the University's mission by disseminating knowledge in the pursuit of education, learning, and research at the highest international levels of excellence.

www.cambridge.org
Information on this title: www.cambridge.org/9781108816854
DOI: 10.1017/9781108860741

First published 2020

A catalogue record for this publication is available from the British Library.

ISBN 978-1-108-81685-4 Paperback
ISSN 2398-4023 (online)
ISSN 2514-3794 (print)

Images as Data for Social Science Research
An Introduction to Convolutional Neural Nets for Image Classification

Elements in Quantitative and Computational Methods for the Social Sciences

DOI: 10.1017/9781108860741
First published online: July 2020

Nora Webb Williams
University of Illinois Urbana-Champaign
Andreu Casas
Vrije Universiteit Amsterdam
John D. Wilkerson
University of Washington

Author for correspondence: Nora Webb Williams, nww3@illinois.edu

Abstract: Images play a crucial role in shaping and reflecting political life. Digitization has vastly increased the presence of such images in daily life, creating valuable new research opportunities for social scientists. We show how recent innovations in computer vision methods can substantially lower the costs of using images as data. We introduce readers to the deep learning algorithms commonly used for object recognition, facial recognition, and visual sentiment analysis. We then provide guidance and specific instructions for scholars interested in using these methods in their own research.

Keywords: political methodology, images as data, machine learning, convolutional neural nets

ISBNs: 9781108816854 (PB), 9781108860741 (OC)
ISSNs: 2398-4023 (online), 2514-3794 (print)

Contents

1 Introduction

Digital photography and the internet have contributed to an explosion in the production and consumption of images in social and political life. According to the Internet Live Stats website,[1] on September 18, 2018, Instagram users were uploading 869 images per second. That works out to 75,081,600 images uploaded per day to just one of many social media platforms. Facebook, Twitter, Snapchat, YouTube, and other sites also enable users to effortlessly share their photos so easily snapped using camera-equipped smartphones as well as computer-generated graphics or memes.

The study of images in social and political life is not new. For example, prior research has established that images play key agenda-setting and framing roles in newspaper coverage (Gitlin 1980; Corrigall-Brown and Wilkes 2012; Brantner, Lobinger, and Irmgard 2011; Powell et al. 2015), that they can influence people's perceptions of political candidates and their votes (S. W. Rosenberg et al. 1986; Todorov et al. 2005); and inspire (or discourage) political participation (Raiford 2007; Casas and Webb Williams 2018; Kharroub and Bas 2015). More generally, a large literature shows that visuals do a better job than written and spoken content in capturing people's attention (Dahmen 2012), facilitating information processing (Grabe and Bucy 2009; Messaris and Abraham 2001), improving information recall (Nelson, Reed, and Walling 1976; Paivio, Rogers, and Smythe 1968), and evoking emotions (Iyer and Oldmeadow 2006).

The abundance of images, however, is new. The presence of so much image content presents both promises and challenges for social scientists. The potential benefits for social science of working with large quantities of digitized images are myriad. Digitized images allow us to test existing theories in new ways and also push us to develop new theories of how image can impact society. Some scholars have already begun delving into using images-as-data, and these studies can be roughly organized into two broad categories: images-as-data in a causal framework and images-as-data for measurement.[2] The borders between these two categories of research using images-as-data are fuzzy, but we nonetheless find the distinction helpful in organizing published and ongoing work.

In a causal framework, images are either the independent or dependent variable (or both). Some prior studies use images as outcome (dependent) variable.

---

[1] www.internetlivestats.com/, last accessed April 26, 2020 (*Internet Live Stats – Internet Usage & Social Media Statistics* 2020).

[2] Yilang Peng maintains a very helpful list of social science papers using computer vision methods at https://yilangpeng.com/computer-vision/, last accessed April 26, 2020 (Y. Peng 2020).

For example, Joo, Li, et al. (2014) show how the choice of visuals can be a means of communicating the intent of politicians. Peng (2018) shows that news outlets choose pictures of political candidates that match the ideological leanings of the outlet. Similarly, Torres (2019) finds that ideological leanings of news outlets are linked to their choices of images to represent stories about the Black Lives Matter movement.

Other studies in the causal framework use images as explanatory (independent) variables, examining how visual inputs relate to some attitudinal or behavioral outcome of interest. For example, in Casas and Webb Williams (2018), we find that images that evoke enthusiasm and fear result in higher rates of online social movement attention and diffusion (measured by retweets) in the context of a Black Lives Matter protest. In another example, Horiuchi, Komatsu, and Nakaya (2012), using automated image analysis, find that the size of candidate smiles in campaign imagery is positively associated with electoral vote shares. Similarly, Joo, Steen, and Zhu (2015) find that candidates' facial traits can predict both party identification and vote share.

Images may also serve as a tool for measurement. Studies in this vein use images not as a treatment or outcome *per se*, but as a source of data providing evidence for another concept of interest. For examples, pictures have been used as evidence of potential electoral incidents (Mebane et al. 2017), and as evidence of tampering in vote counts (Callen and Long 2015; Cantú 2019). Image analysis can be used to detect meaningful corners in legislative districts as a possible proxy measure for compactness (Kaufman, King, and Komisarchik 2019). Lam et al. (2019) use automated image analysis to show differences in the rates of representation of women and men in news stories. Won, Steinert-Threlkeld, and Joo (2017) track protests and estimate their rates of violence using images shared on Twitter, while Steinert-Threlkeld and Joo (n.d.) extract events from images. Similarly, Zhang and Pan (2019) use a combination of images and text to track collective action events. Images can provide estimates of crowd size (Sobolev et al. n.d.). Philipp, Müller-Crepon, and Cederman (n.d.) develop a technique of image segmentation to extract data about road quality from digitized historical maps. Anastasopoulos et al. (2016) analyze images of politicians with constituents of different races in order to understand congressional homestyles. And scholars of political economy and economic development increasingly use nighttime satellite images as a proxy for development (see, for example, Henderson, Storeygard, and Weil 2012; Jean et al. 2016), where a brighter footprint indicates a better-off town or village.

In both the causal and measurement approaches to large-n images-as-data research, a significant challenge is how to accurately and efficiently extract information about the content of an image. This process is variously referred to as classifying, labeling, tagging, annotating or other, more task-specific terms (e.g., image segmentation). The goal is to identify features of interest about or in an image. For example, a researcher might wish to know which photos include a specific object (a flag, perhaps) or a specific individual (perhaps a politician or opposition leader). Or they might want to label images for the reactions or emotions they evoke in viewers. Until recently, scholars interested in such information relied on human annotators, which can be expensive and slow. Computer vision methods now enable any researcher with some programming ability to label large quantities of images more efficiently.

In this Element, we provide code and example data in addition to the text (see Section 2 for details). We use running examples from a corpus of images related to the Black Lives Matter movement that were collected on Twitter for the Casas and Webb Williams (2018) article. Section 5 contains a detailed discussion of the original study and the data. At a high level, our goal was to determine which features of images were tied to higher rates of social movement attention and diffusion. The challenge was labeling a large number of images (around 9,500) on multiple dimensions to disentangle multiple theoretical mechanisms. Here we demonstrate how we could use deep learning to develop classifiers that can automatically label images for multiple features of interest, dramatically reducing manual annotation costs. In the next section we discuss three general labeling tasks that are of particular interest to social scientists and that are also relevant to our specific corpus of Black Lives Matter images and our research goals in that project.

1.1 Three Applications of Computer Vision for Social Scientists

Most cutting-edge computer vision work today relies on Convolutional Neural Nets (abbreviated as CNNs or CovNets). A CNN is given images with known labels to learn from (or *train on*), and then its accuracy is evaluated on a set of held-out validation or test images (again with known labels). In theory, artificial intelligence (AI) computer vision algorithms, either CNNs or other frameworks, can be trained to predict any attribute of an image. This naturally has many potential applications for social science: we could predict how large a crowd is from an image, for example, or guess whether or not the image has been altered. In practice, some labeling tasks are much easier than others. The first two tasks described below, object recognition and facial recognition, can usually (but not always) be accomplished with high accuracy given sufficient and representative training data. The third general task, visual sentiment analysis, is more difficult for reasons that help to illustrate some current limitations of computer vision methods as well as future opportunities.

1.1.1 Object Recognition and Variants

One of the earliest challenges of computer vision research was to successfully distinguish between images of two objects: cats and dogs (e.g., Golle 2008). This type of computer vision task is referred to as *object recognition*. CNNs can now accurately label a wide range of objects, including distinguishing among breeds of cats and dogs and even fish species. The object being recognized does not have to be a solo autonomous entity, however. In our Black Lives Matter study, for example, we wanted to automatically identify (or recognize) whether or not an image was of a street protest. This type of broader object recognition is occasionally referred to as "scene" recognition.

A CNN trained to recognize or classify objects can be either binary (is this an image of a flag or not?) or multiclass (is this an image of a flag, or a cat, or a protest?). Figure 1.1 provides several multiclass image labeling results along with their probabilities from one of the very first successful implementations of a CNN for object recognition (Krizhevsky, Sutskever, and Hinton 2012).

A variant of object recognition is *object detection*. In object detection, the goal is to label the different objects in an image rather than assign a single label to the whole image. Does the image have a cat in it? A dog? A person? Object recognition tasks ask, "What is this a picture of?" while object detection tasks ask, "What things are in this picture?"

A CNN trained to detect objects will also generally provide a bounding box indicating where in the image each object is located. *Object segmentation*, another common and related image analysis task, is similar to object detection but is more precise – instead of generating a bounding box, segmentation should extract the exact outlines of the object (the object "mask"). Figure 1.2 provides a visual for the differences between object classification/recognition,

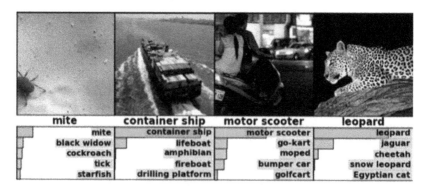

mite	container ship	motor scooter	leopard
mite	container ship	motor scooter	leopard
black widow	lifeboat	go-kart	jaguar
cockroach	amphibian	moped	cheetah
tick	fireboat	bumper car	snow leopard
starfish	drilling platform	golfcart	Egyptian cat

Figure 1.1 Object Recognition using a CNN trained with ImageNet data (from Krizhevsky, Sutskever, and Hinton 2012)

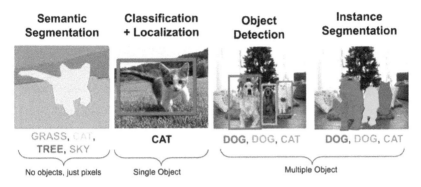

Figure 1.2 The differences between object recognition, detection, and segmentation

Source: Stanford cs231 course, reproduced with permission from Justin Johnson.

localization (a bounding box for a single object), object detection, and segmentation (of either the instance/objects in the image or semantic where each pixel is assigned a meaning).

The prediction of a bounding box or image mask provides additional information that may be of use for social scientists. For example, for a CNN trained to recognize people, we might want to use the bounding boxes to count the number of people present in an image. Or we might be able to discern the location of a particular object type (a flag, for example) across various images. Is the flag consistently in the middle of the image or is it always off to the right? For more on object detection/segmentation research and recent advances with CNNs, see Girshick (2015), Girshick et al. (2013), He, Gkioxari, et al. (2017), and Ren et al. (2015). CNNs are not the only framework for object recognition and variants. For example, a different approach by Redmon, Divvala, et al. (2016) has recently gained popularity for object detection.

In this book, we demonstrate an application of object recognition using the Black Lives Matter image corpus. Our aim is to develop a binary classifier that can automatically and accurately predict whether or not a given picture is of a protest. Depending on the particular theories that a researcher wishes to test, object recognition along these lines could be very valuable. A researcher could automatically label images for the presence or absence of police, for example, or for "I Voted" stickers.

1.1.2 Facial Recognition, Analysis, and Detection

Another class of automated image analysis focuses on faces in images. Facial *recognition* algorithms are trained to answer the question, "Who is this?" Face

Figure 1.3 Li et al.'s 2015 Face Detection algorithm (from Li et al. 2015)

detection, like object detection, picks out where faces are within an image (see Figure 1.3). This is a growing area of research where new methods are proving very accurate (Anastasopoulos et al. 2016; Li et al. 2015; Zhu and Ramanan 2012). Facial *analysis* algorithms predict general features of faces in images such as gender, age, race, or expressed emotion.

One application of facial recognition and facial detection is to identify specific individuals in images. In social science research, one use of facial recognition could be to identify and analyze politicians or other celebrity figures in images. When two politicians from the same party are photographed, are they more likely to smile at one another? Do their facial expressions predict party rifts? Tracking celebrities or politicians is one area where existing image repositories can be very helpful for training classifiers. An example is Guo et al.'s (Guo et al. 2016) compilation of celebrities. It can also be relatively easy to collect what are in effect prelabeled images of celebrities by searching for images of specific individuals online. In this Element we demonstrate a binary facial recognition classifier using images labeled for whether or not they include the singer John Legend (who appeared often in our Black Lives Matter images). John Legend could shape support for the Black Lives Matter movement because he is a popular celebrity and potential opinion leader. To measure the effect of his pictures on support, we need to know which pictures include his face.

Moving away from the Black Lives Matter example, we also demonstrate a multiclass facial recognition example that can distinguish between images of world leaders. This has potential applications for international relations and comparative politics scholars. If we can quickly identify public leaders in images, especially leaders who might not be included in standard celebrity taggers, we could potentially use that information to, for example, predict changes in trade agreements or breakdowns in ceasefires. If leaders are pictured glowering at one another, that may not bode well for peaceful, productive relations.

In our examples, the images of John Legend and world leaders are all close-ups of faces without much else in the picture. To detect the presence of a specific celebrity or world leader in a more complicated image, such as a crowd of people, a researcher would first *detect* (or segment) the different faces in the image before applying a facial *recognition* algorithm to each of the parsed faces. For a recent study that follows this general strategy of face detection and then analysis, see Lam et al. (2019).

1.1.3 Visual Sentiment Analysis and Affect

There are at least two distinct ways to think about emotions and images. The first type of emotional content is the emotion being *expressed* by people in an image. For example, is the individual in the image happy, sad, confused, and so on? Predicting the emotion on a face falls into the category of facial analysis described earlier. The second type of emotional content is the emotion that an image *evokes* in the viewer of the image. Does the image make the viewer feel happy, sad, confused, and so on?

Both of these very different objectives are sometimes called visual sentiment analysis (VSA), although some scholars refer to the latter objective as predicting *affect*. These are very different labeling tasks and are generally more challenging than object detection or facial recognition, in part because emotions are subjective. Accurately predicting *expressed* emotions is the easier of the two sentiment tasks, but even so the task is not as easy as saying whether or not a picture has a puppy in it. *Evoked* emotions, the focus of our VSA examples, are even more subjective. Images can evoke very different responses in different people because of how the viewer filters the information contained in the image. A photo of Donald Trump will evoke very different emotions depending on one's party affiliation, for example.

CNNs now do a moderately good job of predicting evoked emotions for a variety of images (60–70% accuracy) (Peng et al. 2015; You et al. 2015). However, existing analyses are typically based on very clean images of limited scope (see Figure 1.4 for examples). In addition, as with any automated classification task, the results are only as good or as relevant as the training data. Whether an

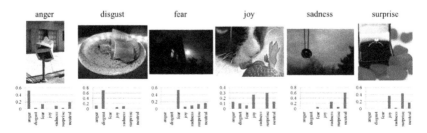

Figure 1.4 Visual Sentiment Analysis using CNN (from Peng et al. 2015)

algorithm trained to predict evoked emotions on one set of images (such as Cornell's Emotion6 from Peng et al. 2015) will do a good job of predicting evoked emotions in other contexts is an open (and very interesting) question. Nevertheless, we view this as one of the most intriguing applications of computer vision methods for social science. Emotions may be a central factor explaining why people are attracted to images, and in turn why images appear to be such powerful forms of communication. One of the questions we asked in the motivating Black Lives Matter study, for example, was whether tweets that evoked emotions such as enthusiasm, disgust, or fear are more likely to be shared (Casas and Webb Williams 2018). In this Element, we test if we can accurately predict human-generated evoked emotions labels using a CNN. While we do not achieve highly accurate results, we still present them here as a demonstration of the challenges, promise, and potential limitations of automated image analysis.

1.2 Other Computer Vision Tasks

The above are just three examples of computer vision tasks that are relevant for social scientists. Computer vision is a very large field. New applications, from automated image captioning to generating fake images, appear in academic journals and the popular press on a regular basis. For example, the aim of optical character recognition (OCR) is to extract text from images (e.g., Kulkarni et al. 2013). This is particularly valuable for studying digitized images in that people increasingly embed text in images (such as memes or screenshots of text used to circumvent Twitter's character limit). Commercial image autotagging services such as Amazon's Rekognition (described in more detail below) often offer text recognition options. An open-source Python option is Tesseract[3] (Smith 2007). Extracting handwriting, as opposed to printed text, is also potentially relevant to social scientists.

Video analysis is another relevant computer vision task for social scientists – each frame of a video can be treated as an image for analysis. Automatically analyzing video data has useful implications for many social science applications. In political science, researchers have begun using computer vision techniques to evaluate facial expressions and body language during debates (Joo, Bucy, and Seidel 2019), process campaign ads (Hwang, Imai, and Tarr 2019), and estimate party polarization (Dietrich 2019).

Dimensionality reduction is another arm of computer vision research of use to social scientists. These techniques take different approaches to reducing complicated pixel interactions into a lower dimensional space. The lower

---

dimensional representation can then be used for automated image clustering and other methods (see, for example, Casas, Webb Williams, et al. [2019]). A full description of these techniques is beyond the scope of this Element, however.

Although we do not explicitly demonstrate the full possible range of computer vision tasks and social science applications in this Element, the CNN logic and processes we do discuss provide an introduction to the field that will be relevant for further reading on automated image analysis and images-as-data (though we hasten to emphasize that not all applications are based on CNNs).

1.3 Overview of the Element

This Element is a practical introduction to computer vision methods for image classification using CNNs, including object recognition, face recognition, and visual sentiment analysis. It is written for social scientists who have some experience with programming languages such as R or Python. We wish to again stress that computer vision is a large and growing field, and that there are relevant tools for social science beyond CNNs and image classification. There are many available books, guides, courses, and free online materials that cover various aspects of computer vision. Most of these are geared toward computer science audiences, so this Element is intended to bring social scientists up to speed on the basics. We hope that this introduction will serve as a springboard for social scientists interested in using computer vision methods in their own images-as-data work.

One extremely helpful advance in image classification is the existence of huge, labeled repositories of images. These repositories are not without controversy, particularly surrounding the sources of the images and possible privacy violations (see Metz 2019 and Section 8 for more). Some previous benchmark datasets may no longer be available because of these concerns. Competitions to build the most accurate classifiers for standard image repositories have resulted in a plethora of trained supervised learning algorithms that can accurately predict the known labels. Many of these trained CNNs are open source. As a result, other researchers can now borrow trained CNNs available commercially or in open-source libraries. As we demonstrate, it is also relatively easy for researchers to adapt these existing algorithms to new purposes (i.e., to assign a different set of labels than those that are in the original benchmark image repository). Whereas the original algorithm may have been the product of many months of effort using millions of labeled examples, this *fine-tuning* or *transfer learning* can produce remarkably accurate results using a much smaller training set of images (as few as 100 in some cases).

CNNs are a specialized type of deep learning algorithm. They take as raw data the values of each pixel in a digitized image, generally either red, green, and blue (RGB) values or grayscale. They use lots of prelabeled training images to "learn" which pixel combinations are associated with the desired labels. An algorithm's accuracy is assessed by applying it to prelabeled validation or test images that are not included in the training set. Once performance is satisfactory, the algorithm can then be used to label large numbers of additional images quickly and at very low cost.

In this Element we do not focus on the process of training a CNN classifier from scratch (although we do discuss how artificial and convolutional neural networks work), as this usually requires a very large number of manually labeled images and lots of computational power. A social science researcher looking to label images using what might be considered "conventional" labels (e.g., whether the picture contains basic objects like cats, dogs, cars, or motorcycles) does not need to know how to build their own new classifier. They can simply use one of many available off-the-shelf trained algorithms (either commercial or open source) that are optimized for these labels. We provide a brief introduction to one commercial service (Amazon's Rekognition) as one of these "autotagger" options. However, rarely are social scientists interested in these conventional labels. Hence, our primary focus is on fine-tuning, where the objective is to adapt or "fine-tune" an existing algorithm to assign a specific set of labels developed by a researcher. With these tools, new subfields of social science are in the making.

The remainder of this Element proceeds as follows. In Section 2 we first discuss some technical requirements for the methods described in this Element. While computer vision methods have become increasingly accessible, there are some prerequisites to using the techniques we describe. In Section 3, we provide an introduction to the basics of deep learning and CNNs. Section 4 describes the main method we advance in this book, fine-tuning a CNN, with subsections on image preprocessing, hyperparameters, and diagnostics.

Turning from theory to application, Section 5 introduces the data (images) used in our examples. As part of an earlier project, we collected and labeled 9,500 unique images shared on Twitter by people tweeting about a Black Lives Matter (BLM) protest. We then labeled the images for select content and for the emotions they evoked in viewers. The example applications evaluate the degree to which we can successfully predict the manual labels using automated means.

One way to leverage the deep learning revolution for image analysis is to use off-the-shelf autotaggers, many of which are based on CNNs. In Section 6 we use some of the BLM images to demonstrate both the promise and the limits of autotaggers. We provide example code to use one of many available commercial autotagging services: Amazon's Rekognition.

Given the many limitations of autotaggers, many social scientists will likely decide that fine-tuning an existing classifier is the best option for their classification tasks. Section 7 explains the technical details of fine-tuning, along with a series of binary examples and a multiclass example. Working with the BLM data, we demonstrate how to fine-tune a CNN to predict the presence of protest, the presence of John Legend, and whether or not an image evokes one of five emotions. We then draw on a separate toy dataset to demonstrate a multiclass model predicting images of six world leaders.

In Section 8 we raise but do not fully answer some thorny legal and ethical questions related to training computer vision algorithms and using images obtained from sources such as social media in research. While we have few definitive answers to these questions, we do suggest resources and advise our fellow scholars to incorporate discussions of ethics into every part of their research pipelines, including data collection, analysis, and publication.

2 Prerequisites for Computer Vision Methods and Tutorials

This Element includes interactive, well-commented tutorials and example code designed to make the process of using CNNs for image labeling more comprehensible and accessible. Most of our visualizations and tables are written in R (primarily drawing on the tidyverse package from Wickham [2017]), while most of the computer vision scripts are written in Python. Python 3.5 and higher have well-supported computer vision packages. Users of Python 2.7 may find that needed packages (dependencies) are not available. Python also offers additional benefits for computer vision research. Services such as Amazon's Mechanical Turk can be accessed using Python, making it possible to automate the processes of recruiting and paying image annotators for gold-standard labels. Automatic image tagger APIs (application program interfaces) from Amazon, Google, and Microsoft are also accessible via Python.

Readers can replicate and modify our analyses by using the companion Code Ocean capsule,[4] which includes sample images. Code Ocean is a site for hosting code, data, and computing environments and is primarily designed for replication purposes. A benefit of Code Ocean is that users can run code on the platform for free. Since each capsule provides information about the computing requirements for the project (e.g., which versions of packages to use, any required hardware), this removes one of the major hurdles for replication. For

---

[4] https://doi.org/10.24433/CO.2462313.v1, last accessed April 26, 2020 (Webb Williams, Casas, and Wilkerson 2020).

advanced users, note that the Code Ocean capsule contains an environment directory with a Docker file. However, Code Ocean users are subject to computing quotas. To get started on Code Ocean, create an account (using a .edu email address will give you a higher computing quota) and then navigate to the accompanying Code Ocean capsule.[5] To run or edit the code, create a private copy of the capsule (there are many options to do this, from clicking on "Edit Capsule" or "Re-Run" to selecting "Duplicate" from the "Capsule" drop-down menu). Once you have a private copy, you can start a cloud computing session by clicking on "Launch Cloud Workstation" – for our project, we recommend using the Jupyter option. Once the cloud machine launches, you can edit and rerun the code in a Jupyter Notebook (see the official Jupyter site[6] for an introduction to Jupyter Notebooks).

While Code Ocean is an excellent resource for replication and slight modifications, due to computing quotas it may not be the best framework for extensive edits or for implementing the demonstrated methods on a different set of images for a different classification scheme. For these reasons, scholars may wish to edit and run the code elsewhere. Code Ocean gives users the option to "Export" the capsule for other uses. We also make the replication files available in a Github repository[7] for those more familiar with that platform (Github is primarily for storing and sharing code).

Training CNNs can require substantial computing power. Graphics processing units (GPUs) increase efficiency. When readers run the provided scripts using Code Ocean, their cloud computing sessions will run on a GPU-equipped machine. However, researchers who would like to adapt these scripts for other purposes will likely need their own high-performance machines, access to high-performing computer clusters through their institutions, or access to a commercial cloud computing instance.

The code provided in this Element was initially run on the Amazon Web Services (AWS) cloud computing platform known as EC2, and some of our accompanying tutorials are built for this service, but there are other commercial cloud computing platforms available (e.g., Microsoft's Azure and Google Cloud). An EC2 instance is essentially a remote computer that researchers can access over the Internet and use to run code. Renting an EC2 instance can cost anywhere from $0.0052 to $24.48 per hour, depending on the type

---

[5] https://doi.org/10.24433/CO.2462313.v1, last accessed April 26, 2020 (Webb Williams, Casas, and Wilkerson 2020).

[6] https://jupyter.org/, last accessed April 26, 2020 (*Project Jupyter | Home* 2020).

[7] https://github.com/norawebbwilliams/images_as_data, last accessed April 26, 2020 (Webb Williams and Casas 2020).

of machine.[8] EC2 instances do not have keyboards or monitors – to interact with them requires some comfort using the command line (or bash terminal). One advantage of replicating our AWS infrastructure for your own applications is that the setup will have the correct hardware and package versions for the scripts accompanying this Element. Detailed instructions for setting up such an AWS instance are provided in a guide on the accompanying Github.[9]

Supervised learning algorithms such as CNNs require labeled images for training and validation purposes. In this Element we devote little attention to methods for obtaining images (such as how to use social media APIs; see, for example, Steinert-Threlkeld [2018]), for creating annotated training sets, and for data collection and storage. Procedures and performance metrics for qualitative coding are well developed (see Saldaña [2009]), and researchers have several options for generating original labels. Undergraduate and graduate students have long been a staple of such work. Services such as LabelBox and Atlas.ti offer infrastructure for efficiently managing labeling projects. Crowdsourcing services, such as Amazon's Mechanical Turk or Figure Eight (formerly Crowdflower), are used widely in computer vision label generation (and text-as-data work – see Benoit et al. [2016] for an excellent application and discussion of the strengths and limitations of crowdsourcing services).

Researchers also have the option of using benchmark image datasets that typically include lots of images with well-validated labels. A careful Internet search for potential training data may end up saving a lot of time. However, the images and labels in these datasets may be of limited value if they are not representative of the images or labels of interest. An example that we will return to is images of protests. If existing image repositories do not include images labeled as protests, it will be impossible for a CNN trained on that data to recognize protests. But even repositories that do include labeled protest images may not suffice. Images of Arab Spring protests, for example, may or may not be good training data for a project that seeks to identify Tea Party protests.

Data storage can become an issue in computer vision research because digitized image files can be quite large. Cloud storage services (such as Amazon's S3, Google Drive, Dropbox, or academic institution-specific services) now provide virtually unlimited storage (at a cost). Commercial services are usually also accessible by API. For larger, long-term projects (involving terabytes of data), it may be more cost effective to purchase physical hard drives.

---

[8] For latest pricing, see https://aws.amazon.com/ec2/pricing/on-demand/, last accessed April 26, 2020.

[9] https://github.com/norawebbwilliams/images_as_data/blob/master/notes/01-launch-use-ec2-aws-instances.md, last accessed April 26, 2020 (Webb Williams and Casas 2020).

Finally, we urge readers to constantly consider the privacy and ethics implications of their image data collection, labeling, and sharing practices. Are we paying workers fairly? Are we causing harm by asking students or crowdsourcing workers to label potentially offensive or graphic images? Do our strategies for storing and sharing data respect individual privacy? We discuss these issues in more depth in Section 8.

In the Section 3, we look "under the hood" of deep learning algorithms. Before fine-tuning a CNN, we need some understanding of how they work. What is a deep learning Artificial Neural Network (ANN)? And why does most computer vision research rely on CNNs?

3 Introduction to CNNs for Social Scientists

As the applications described earlier demonstrate, the field of computer vision has grown by leaps and bounds in the last decade. Today most, but not all, computer vision research is based on CNNs (or ConvNets), a type of "deep learning" neural network that works well with images as inputs. Convolutional nets can also be used for other data types, including text (Britz 2015). In this section we describe the basics of deep learning (beginning with ANNs), CNNs, and CNNs for image analysis. For additional information about these subjects, we highly recommend Buduma and Locascio (2017)'s book and the materials accompanying Stanford University's CS231n course.[10]

ANNs are statistical models that use what are called *intermediate abstract representations* (or *hidden layers*) of the input data (any data matrix, known as the *input layer*) to learn from new features in those hidden layers and better predict outcomes. The intermediate representations result from applying a large number of complex interactions and nonlinear transformations to the initial input matrix. "Deep learning" refers to the presence of multiple hidden layers.

As a toy example to demonstrate an ANN, suppose that we wanted to predict the vote share for Hillary Clinton during the 2016 Democratic primaries as a function of some county-level features, using the data from seven California counties displayed in Table 3.1 (data source: 2016 U.S. Election Kaggle competition, Hamner [2019]). We would start with a 7×4 input matrix X containing information about the percentage of the county population that is white (x_1), the percentage of the county population with at least a college education (x_2), the median income per capita (x_3), as well as an intercept column (x_0). The goal would be to use this information to predict Clinton's vote share, contained in a 7×1 output matrix Y. In conventional machine learning, we could estimate

---

[10] http://cs231n.stanford.edu/, last accessed April 26, 2020 (*CS231n Convolutional Neural Networks for Visual Recognition* 2020).

Table 3.1 Vote share for Hillary Clinton in the 2016 Democratic primaries in seven California counties.

County	White (%)	College (%)	Median Income (per capita, in hundreds USD)	Vote Share
Lake	87.70	16.20	215.37	0.46
Shasta	88.50	18.80	236.70	0.48
Mendocino	86.30	22.00	233.06	0.36
Sonoma	87.40	32.20	328.35	0.51
Sutter	74.00	18.70	236.02	0.55
Amador	90.70	19.30	273.47	0.52
Napa	84.80	31.30	347.95	0.60

$$
\overset{X}{\begin{matrix} x_0 & x_1 & x_2 & x_3 \end{matrix}} \\
\begin{bmatrix}
1 & 87.7 & 16.2 & 215.37 \\
1 & 88.5 & 18.8 & 236.70 \\
1 & 86.3 & 22.0 & 233.06 \\
1 & 87.4 & 32.2 & 328.35 \\
1 & 74.0 & 18.7 & 236.02 \\
1 & 90.7 & 19.3 & 273.47 \\
1 & 84.8 & 31.3 & 347.95
\end{bmatrix}
\times
\overset{\beta}{\begin{bmatrix}
0.6423 \\
-0.0066 \\
-0.0184 \\
0.0031
\end{bmatrix}}
=
\overset{\hat{Y}}{\begin{bmatrix}
0.43 \\
0.45 \\
0.39 \\
0.49 \\
0.54 \\
0.54 \\
0.59
\end{bmatrix}}
\qquad (1)
$$

Figure 3.1 A linear model predicting Clinton's vote share in the 2016 Democratic primaries in seven California counties ($\hat{Y}$), as a function of the percentage of white population (x_1), people with college education (x_2), and the median income per capita (x_3).

(for example) a simple linear model ($Y = X\beta$) by finding the 4×1 coefficient matrix β that minimizes predictive error (the difference between actual Ys and predicted $\hat{Y}$s). Figure 3.1 presents this linear model in matrix format. Importantly, only one parameter is associated with each input variable. For example, in Figure 3.1 the blue coefficient ($\beta_{12} = -0.0066$) describes the best association between the percentage of whites in a county (x_1) and the results: all else being equal, the model predicts that Clinton's vote share will be 0.0066 percentage point lower when the percentage of whites increases by 1 point.

If we are more interested in accurately predicting the results of the Democratic primaries than in interpreting or understanding the specific effects of race, education, and wealth, we might want to to use a "deep learning" artificial neural network to improve accuracy. Studies demonstrate that neural nets can achieve higher predictive accuracy for a wide range of tasks (LeCun, Bengio, and Hinton 2015). The main difference between conventional machine learning algorithms and artificial neural networks is that there is more than one parameter associated with each input variable. The initial input variables are transformed into new abstract representations, and coefficients are estimated for these intermediate representations as well as for the original inputs. These intermediate representations result from multiple interactions and nonlinear transformations. Importantly, unlike in the initial example, the coefficients from deep learning models are rarely interpretable in the sense that social scientists are used to. The hidden layers tend to be black boxes (though making these models more interpretable by humans is a growing computer #science field).

Basic matrix multiplication (or a dot product) is one of the keys to understanding artificial neural networks. In particular, in order to be able to multiply two matrices, (a) the number of rows in the first matrix needs to be the same as the number of columns in the second one, and (b) the resulting matrix will have the same number of rows as the first matrix and the same number of columns as the second matrix. The dot products between data matrices and parameter (*coefficient* or *weight*) matrices are what facilitate transforming original inputs into new abstract representations (or "hidden layers"). The hidden layers represent the information in the input layer in a new way, offering new learning opportunities that can improve predictive accuracy.

Figure 3.2 uses the running example from Figure 3.1 to illustrate an artificial neural network. In Figure 3.2(1) we transform the original 7×4 input layer X into a 7×2 hidden layer Z_0 by multiplying the input by a 4×2 weights matrix β_1 (the red entries highlight these matrix multiplication steps). This dot product allows for multiple varied interactions of the input variables, and the weights matrix β_1 estimates the effect of these multiple interactions. Then it is common practice to apply a nonlinear transformation to this new hidden layer. Such transformations are well known to improve model fit and predictive power by accounting for nonlinear relationships between input and output (Gelman and Hill [2007], Ch. 4). In Figure 3.2(2) we apply a ReLu (Rectified Linear Unit, where negative values are replaced by 0s) to the hidden layer Z_0, creating a new version of the same layer: Z_1. Several nonlinear transformations (known as *activation functions*) are commonly used in deep learning models. Figure 3.3 illustrates the properties of three common activation functions by transforming a set of original values between -5 and 5. Each method has its pros and cons,[11] but Krizhevsky, Sutskever, and Hinton (2012) find that applying ReLu (rather than sigmoid or tanh) transformations to hidden layers accelerates

[11] See these notes for more details: http://cs231n.github.io/neural-networks-1/#actfun, last accessed April 26, 2020 via *CS231n Convolutional Neural Networks for Visual Recognition* (2020).

(Input Layer: 7×4)

X

$$\begin{bmatrix} 1 & 87.7 & 16.2 & 215.37 \\ 1 & 88.5 & 18.8 & 236.70 \\ 1 & 86.3 & 22.0 & 233.06 \\ 1 & 87.4 & 32.2 & 328.35 \\ 1 & 74.0 & 18.7 & 236.02 \\ 1 & 90.7 & 19.3 & 273.47 \\ 1 & 84.8 & 31.3 & 347.95 \end{bmatrix} \times$$

(Weights: 4×2)

β_1

$$\begin{bmatrix} 0.4634 & -0.3303 \\ -0.1495 & 0.1094 \\ -0.6841 & -0.0567 \\ 0.1183 & -0.3340 \end{bmatrix} =$$

(Hidden Layer 1 nontransformed: 7×2)

Z_0

$$\begin{bmatrix} 1.7436 & -63.6019 \\ 2.3684 & -70.7870 \\ 0.0775 & -69.9929 \\ 4.2065 & -102.2821 \\ 4.5243 & -72.1398 \\ 6.0468 & -82.8577 \\ 7.5294 & -109.0627 \end{bmatrix} \quad (1)$$

(Hidden Layer 1 transformed)

Z_1

$$max(0, Z_0) = \begin{bmatrix} 1.7436 & 0.0000 \\ 2.3684 & 0.0000 \\ 0.0775 & 0.0000 \\ 4.2065 & 0.0000 \\ 4.5243 & 0.0000 \\ 6.0468 & 0.0000 \\ 7.5294 & 0.0000 \end{bmatrix} \quad (2)$$

(Hidden Layer 1 transformed: 7×3)

Z_1

$$\begin{bmatrix} 1 & 1.7436 & 0.0000 \\ 1 & 2.3684 & 0.0000 \\ 1 & 0.0775 & 0.0000 \\ 1 & 4.2065 & 0.0000 \\ 1 & 4.5243 & 0.0000 \\ 1 & 6.0468 & 0.0000 \\ 1 & 7.5294 & 0.0000 \end{bmatrix} \times$$

(Weights: 3×1)

β_2

$$\begin{bmatrix} -0.4142 \\ 0.1084 \\ -0.1024 \end{bmatrix} =$$

(Output Layer nontransformed: 7×1)

$\hat{Y}_0$

$$\begin{bmatrix} -0.2252 \\ -0.1575 \\ -0.4058 \\ 0.0418 \\ 0.0762 \\ 0.2412 \\ 0.4019 \end{bmatrix} \quad (3)$$

(Output Layer transformed)

$\hat{Y}_1$

$$\frac{1}{(1+\epsilon^{-\hat{Y}_0})} = \begin{bmatrix} 0.4420 \\ 0.4586 \\ 0.3979 \\ 0.5076 \\ 0.5170 \\ 0.5576 \\ 0.5962 \end{bmatrix} \quad (4)$$

Figure 3.2 An artificial neural network predicting Clinton's vote share in the 2016 Democratic primaries in seven California counties ($\hat{Y}$) as a function of percentage of white population (x_1), people with college education (x_2), the median income per capita (x_3), and an intermediate representation of both (Z_1): (1) using the *input layer* X to create a new *hidden layer* Z_0, (2) applying a nonlinear ReLu transformation to the *hidden layer* Z_0, (3) using the features in the *hidden layer* to generate a set of predictions ($\hat{Y}_0$), and (4) applying a sigmoid transformation to these predictions to improve model fit ($\hat{Y}_1$).

model convergence. Sigmoid and tanh activations can, however, be useful in a final layer, depending on the outcome to be predicted: note in Figure 3.3 that they generate values bounded between 0 and 1, and -1 and 1, respectively.

Then, after adding an intercept column (known as *bias*) to the new matrix Z_1, we multiply the 7×3 hidden layer by a new 3×1 coefficient (weights) matrix β_2 to produce a final 7×1 output layer of model predictions $\hat{Y}_0$. Finally, we

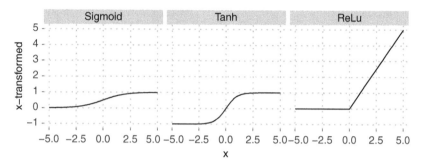

Figure 3.3 Three common nonlinear transformations (*activation functions*) in deep learning.

take advantage of one final nonlinear transformation to improve model fit and predictive power. Rather than using a ReLu, we apply a sigmoid transformation (a special case of the logistic function) to the output layer, which works well for predicting proportions (values bounded between 0 and 1). This last step generates a final set of predictions $\hat{Y}_1$.

Now that we have set the ANN architecture (the number and size of the hidden layers, our choices of activation functions, etc.), the next challenge is to determine what the values of the parameters in each layer should be in order to maximize predictive accuracy (or, in other words, to minimize predictive error). The weights in β_1 and β_2 are first initialized with random values and then learned via Stochastic Gradient Descent (SGD), or variants thereof, and the chain rule is used to derive the gradient. The model is estimated multiple times (*epochs*), each time calculating all of the dot products to generate a new set of predictions (*forward propagation*), then calculating the gradient and updating the weight parameters (*backward propagation*) based on the model loss (the difference between Y and $\hat{Y}_1$), until the loss of subsequent epochs reaches a point of convergence. The values in Figure 3.2 show the values learned after 1,000,000 epochs of the model.

An artificial neural network has as many layers as the number of hidden layers plus the last outcome layer. Thus the previous example (Figure 3.2) is a two-layer-deep network because it has one hidden layer Z plus the outcome layer Y. The ReLu transformation is not counted as a layer because there are no weights to estimate (the same is true for pooling layers, described later). The two layers in the example are also *fully connected* because we apply the dot product to all units of a given layer (e.g., each data row in the input layer X) and each unit of the following layer (e.g., each parameter in the parameter matrix β_1). For additional information about ANNs, see LeCun, Bengio, and Hinton (2015) and Schmidhuber (2015).

3.1 Convolutional Neural Networks

Convolutional neural networks are a type of artificial neural network often used in computer vision research. Their distinguishing characteristic is that, in at least some of the hidden layers, the weights are not fully connected to the whole output of the previous layer. Instead, a weights matrix called a *filter* is connected to only one region of the input at a time. These filters learn features of an image, such as the presence of a line segment or shape. The great advantage of these convolutional layers, compared to fully connected layers, is that they are much easier (and faster) to compute. This becomes particularly important in computer vision because the input matrices for images (three dimensions of pixel information) can be very large.

Figures 3.4(1) and 3.4(2) are similar to 3.2(1) and 3.2(2): an input layer X is transformed into a new hidden layer Z_0, to which we then apply a ReLu nonlinearity (generating Z_1). In 3.4(3) we add a convolutional layer. That is, instead of applying the dot product to the entire hidden layer Z_1 and a new weights matrix, we slide the filter β_2 along Z_1 horizontally and vertically, multiplying the aligned input and weight indices and recording (in K) the sum of the outputs. Figure 3.4(3) highlights in blue the input units involved in the first convolution (0 and 10.0404) as well as the resulting output $((0 \times -0.5090) + (10.0404 \times 0.186) = 18.729)$. The next convolution would shift the filter horizontally $((10.0404 \times -0.5090) + (61.5057 \times 0.186) = 6.3629)$, and vertically $((0 \times -0.5090) + (11.3235 \times 0.186) = 2.1122)$, and so on. The notions of forward and backward propagation remain the same. Figure 3.4 shows the weights learned after 1,000,000 epochs of the model.

3.2 Convolutional Neural Networks for Image Classification

Where images differ from the previous example is in the input layer. Instead of having a matrix of information about counties in California, we have information about pixel intensities. Figure 3.5 illustrates how an image can be represented as a three-dimensional matrix. The relevant features of images are the colors and intensities of their pixels. The three-dimensional matrices (or volumes) correspond to image width and height (in pixels) and color (red, green, and blue [RGB] intensity channels). A typical image could therefore be transformed into a $224 \times 224 \times 3$ input volume X, where, for example, $X_{1,1,1}$ contains information about the red intensity of the pixel in the top-left corner of the image and $X_{1,1,2}$ and $X_{1,1,3}$ contain information about the green and blue intensities of the same pixel, respectively. Each pixel representation $X_{i,j,z}$ is usually a standardized integer ranging from 0 to 255, where higher values indicate stronger intensity of a given color.

(Input Layer: 7×4)
$$X$$
$$\begin{bmatrix} 1 & 87.7 & 16.2 & 215.37 \\ 1 & 88.5 & 18.8 & 236.70 \\ 1 & 86.3 & 22.0 & 233.06 \\ 1 & 87.4 & 32.2 & 328.35 \\ 1 & 74.0 & 18.7 & 236.02 \\ 1 & 90.7 & 19.3 & 273.47 \\ 1 & 84.8 & 31.3 & 347.95 \end{bmatrix}$$

(Fully Connected Weights: 4×3)
$$\beta_1$$
$$\begin{bmatrix} -0.0007 & 0.6163 & -0.3102 \\ -0.4425 & -0.1089 & 0.3600 \\ -0.2725 & -0.5114 & 0.1802 \\ -0.4045 & 0.1266 & 0.1269 \end{bmatrix} =$$

(Hidden Layer 1 nontransformed: 7×3)
$$Z_0$$
$$\begin{bmatrix} -130.3434 & 10.0404 & 61.5057 \\ -140.0340 & 11.3235 & 64.9685 \\ -138.4599 & 9.4660 & 64.2914 \\ -180.2716 & 16.1915 & 78.6155 \\ -133.3151 & 12.8679 & 59.6443 \\ -156.0177 & 15.4824 & 70.5158 \\ -186.8042 & 19.4159 & 80.0041 \end{bmatrix} \quad (1)$$

(Hidden Layer 1 transformed)
$$Z_1$$
$$max(0, Z_0) = \begin{bmatrix} 0 & 10.0404 & 61.5057 \\ 0 & 11.3235 & 64.9685 \\ 0 & 9.4660 & 64.2914 \\ 0 & 16.1915 & 78.6155 \\ 0 & 12.8679 & 59.6443 \\ 0 & 15.4824 & 70.5158 \\ 0 & 19.4159 & 80.0041 \end{bmatrix} \quad (2)$$

(Hidden Layer 1 transformed)
$$Z_1$$
$$\begin{bmatrix} 0 & 10.0404 & 61.5057 \\ 0 & 11.3235 & 64.9685 \\ 0 & 9.4660 & 64.2914 \\ 0 & 16.1915 & 78.6155 \\ 0 & 12.8679 & 59.6443 \\ 0 & 15.4824 & 70.5158 \\ 0 & 19.4159 & 80.0041 \end{bmatrix} *$$

(Convolutional Filter: 1×2)
$$\beta_2$$
$$\begin{bmatrix} -0.5090 & 0.186 \end{bmatrix} =$$

(Hidden Layer 2)
$$K$$
$$\begin{bmatrix} 1.8729 & 6.3629 \\ 2.1122 & 6.3558 \\ 1.7657 & 7.1749 \\ 3.0203 & 6.4238 \\ 2.4003 & 4.5766 \\ 2.8880 & 5.2738 \\ 3.6218 & 5.0418 \end{bmatrix} \quad (3)$$

(Hidden Layer 2: 7×3)
$$K$$
$$\begin{bmatrix} 1 & 1.8729 & 6.3629 \\ 1 & 2.1122 & 6.3558 \\ 1 & 1.7657 & 7.1749 \\ 1 & 3.0203 & 6.4238 \\ 1 & 2.4003 & 4.5766 \\ 1 & 2.8880 & 5.2738 \\ 1 & 3.6218 & 5.0418 \end{bmatrix} \times$$

(Fully Connected Weights: 3×1)
$$\beta_3$$
$$\begin{bmatrix} 0.4660 \\ 0.2257 \\ -0.1782 \end{bmatrix} =$$

(Output Layer nontransformed: 7×1)
$$\hat{Y}_0$$
$$\begin{bmatrix} -0.2450 \\ -0.1897 \\ -0.4139 \\ 0.0031 \\ 0.1923 \\ 0.1782 \\ 0.3852 \end{bmatrix} \quad (4)$$

(Output Layer transformed)
$$\hat{Y}_1$$
$$\frac{1}{(1 + \epsilon^{-\hat{Y}_0})} = \begin{bmatrix} 0.4391 \\ 0.4527 \\ 0.3980 \\ 0.5008 \\ 0.5479 \\ 0.5444 \\ 0.5951 \end{bmatrix} \quad (5)$$

Figure 3.4 Convolutional neural network predicting Clinton's vote share ($\hat{Y}$): (1) using *input layer* X to create a new *hidden layer* (Z_0), (2) applying a ReLu transformation to Z_0, (3) using a 1×2 convolutional filter to create a new hidden layer K, (4) using K to generate a set of predictions ($\hat{Y}_0$), and (5) applying a sigmoid transformation to improve model fit.

Pixel-level information about color intensity is the primary input data used to predict all types of image labels or classifications (the output Y). For example, our dataset could include 50 images of protesting crowds, such as the one in Figure 3.5, and 50 images of other things (e.g., pictures of cats, selfies, soldiers). We could split these 100 true positive and true negative images

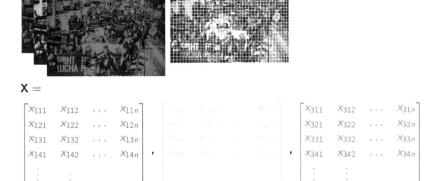

$$\mathbf{X} =$$

$$
\begin{bmatrix}
x_{111} & x_{112} & \cdots & x_{11n} \\
x_{121} & x_{122} & \cdots & x_{12n} \\
x_{131} & x_{132} & \cdots & x_{13n} \\
x_{141} & x_{142} & \cdots & x_{14n} \\
\vdots & \vdots & & \vdots \\
x_{1n1} & x_{1n2} & \cdots & x_{1nn}
\end{bmatrix},
\begin{bmatrix}
 & & & \\
 & & & \\
 & & & \\
 & & & \\
 & & & \\
 & & &
\end{bmatrix},
\begin{bmatrix}
x_{311} & x_{312} & \cdots & x_{31n} \\
x_{321} & x_{322} & \cdots & x_{32n} \\
x_{331} & x_{332} & \cdots & x_{33n} \\
x_{341} & x_{342} & \cdots & x_{34n} \\
\vdots & \vdots & & \vdots \\
x_{3n1} & x_{3n2} & \cdots & x_{3nn}
\end{bmatrix}
$$

Figure 3.5 An image represented as a three-dimensional input. Each $X_{i,j,z}$ unit contains information about the pixel-level intensity of red, green, and blue in the image.

into a train and a validation set, then use the three-dimensional matrix representations of the images as input volumes (X), and train an artificial neural network to predict which ones include protesting crowds ($\hat{Y}$). However, given the three-dimensional nature of the images (each image has over 150,000 features ranging from 0 to 255), an artificial neural network with fully connected layers would take a long time to train, especially one that included several hidden layers.

For this reason, state-of-the-art computer vision algorithms use CNNs instead of fully connected ANNs. Figure 3.6 illustrates how the first convolutional layer of a CNN for image modeling works. On the left side is an image X expressed as a three-dimensional input volume (three matrices of pixel-level red intensities [bottom], green [middle], and blue [top]). This example input volume is of size $5 \times 5 \times 3$, meaning that the example image is 5 pixels wide and 5 pixels tall (instead of a more standard 224×224 pixel size). For this example, we also limit the range of color intensities from 0 to 2 (instead of the usual 0 to 255). The convolutional layer is composed of two $2 \times 2 \times 3$ (β_1 and β_2) filters that we convolve (slide) over the input volume, creating a new $4 \times 4 \times 2$ output volume Z. The first (top) dimension of the first filter β_1 is connected only to the first (blue) channel of the input volume, the second dimension is connected only to the second (green) channel, and the last one is connected only to the red channel. As in Figure 3.4(3), we convolve each of the three dimensions of the β_1 filter through the particular channel to which it is

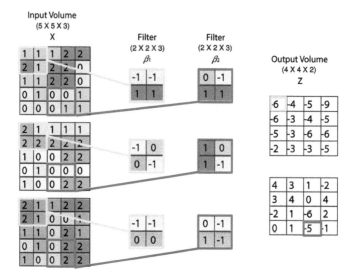

Figure 3.6 An example of a convolutional layer in a CNN for image processing

connected, multiplying in each convolution the aligned input and filter indices, then summing the outputs within the filter, and finally recording (in the output volume) the sum across the three filter dimensions. If desired, we can also use this output volume as the input volume in a new convolutional layer, extending and improving the learning process and model accuracy.

In Figure 3.6, the indices of the input X, of the filter (β_1) performing the convolution, and of the output volume Z involved in the first convolution are highlighted in orange. We multiply and sum up each index of the first dimension of the β_1 filter to the top-left region of the blue channel: $((1 \times -1) + (1 \times -1) + (2 \times 1) + (1 \times 1) = 1)$; each index of the second dimension to the top-left region of the green channel: $((2 \times -1) + (1 \times 0) + (2 \times 0) + (2 \times -1) = -4)$; and each index of the third filter dimension to the top-left region of the red channel: $((2 \times -1) + (1 \times -1) + (2 \times 0) + (1 \times 0) = -3)$. Finally, we record the sum of all these partial outputs (one for each color channel) in the top corner of the output volume (in $Z_{11} = 1 + (-4) + (-3) = -6$). You can also see the input parts, filters, and output value involved in another convolution, highlighted in purple. This animation[12] illustrates the process dynamically.

State-of-the-art CNNs often have convolutional layers with numerous filters (our example in Figure 3.6 has only two), generating output volumes (or hidden layers) of a large size. The advantage of transforming the input

---

[12] http://cs231n.github.io//assets/conv-demo/index.html, last accessed April 26, 2020 via *CS231n Convolutional Neural Networks for Visual Recognition* (2020).

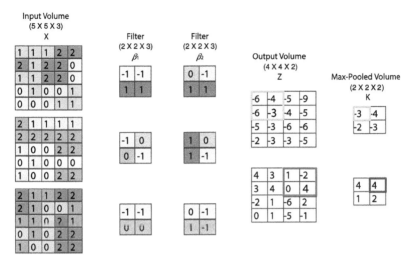

Figure 3.7 A convolutional layer (filters β_1 and β_2 create output volume Z) and a pooling layer (output volume Z is downsampled to Max-Pooled Volume K using the max operator)

image into a high-dimensional volume is that we increase the number of features we can potentially learn from. However, high-dimensional volumes can also be problematic. The number of parameters to learn via stochastic gradient descent and the computational power required to estimate the model may drastically increase, and we risk overfitting the model. To address such concerns, researchers often downsample and reduce the dimensionality of output volumes. These downsampled layers are called *pooling* layers. In Figure 3.7 we add a pooling layer to the convolutional layer of the previous figure. Specifically, we split each of the two Z dimensions into four quadrants (for example, one quadrant of the first dimension $\{-6, -4, -6, -3\}$ is highlighted in orange and another quadrant of the second dimension is highlighted in purple $\{1, -2, 0, 4\}$) and build a new output (Max-Pooled) volume K by taking the maximum value of the quadrants (-3 and 4 respectively for the highlighted quadrants).

In a CNN for image classification, the first layer is always convolutional. Researchers then combine additional convolutional layers with ReLu layers that add nonlinearities, pooling layers (to avoid overfitting and reducing computation time and complexity), and fully connected layers (a set of weights that are connected to all of the input features). The final (usually fully connected) layer reduces the second-to-last layer into a one-dimensional vector equal in size to the number of unique classes to be predicted. A final common step is to transform the final class scores into probabilities that sum to one by attaching a *Softmax* layer (or multinomial model) onto the final fully connected layer.

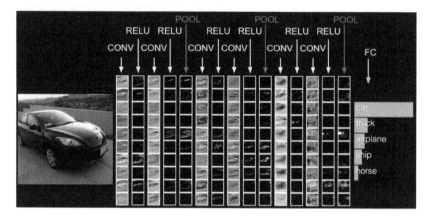

Figure 3.8 An example of an entire CNN for image classification.
Source: Stanford cs231 course, reproduced with permission from Serena Yeung.

Once a CNN has been trained, which means that its parameter values lead to an acceptable predictive accuracy, it can be used to predict the labels of held-out images. Figure 3.8 displays the application of a CNN trained to recognize 1,000 different classes to a new image. The first convolutional layer has 10 filters, generating a 10-dimensional output volume. Additional convolutional layers with 10 filters are combined with ReLu and pooling layers. Finally, a fully connected layer predicts the class of the image, and a softmax layer transforms the unidimensional output into a set of class probabilities. The bar graph on the far right of the figure displays the five highest probability classes. The highest probability class, a car, is the correct prediction in this case.

4 Overview of Fine-Tuning a CNN Classifier for Images

In the previous section, we provided a theoretical overview of what convolutional neural networks are and how they work. In this chapter we address the practicalities of developing a CNN for specific research-driven image classification tasks. Our focus is on explaining how one can reuse a CNN that has already been built and trained on large datasets of images (e.g., trained to classify images into the 1,000 objects that are part of the ImageNet competition) to then build a classifier to perform a new classification task of interest to the researcher. This process is known as *fine-tuning* (or *transfer learning*) and it can more efficiently achieve accurate results than building and training a CNN from scratch (Krizhevsky, Sutskever, and Hinton [2012]). We first explain fine-tuning in detail. Then we describe the preprocessing steps needed to prepare images before feeding them into a CNN. We next explain the range of hyper-parameters involved in the training (and/or fine-tuning) of a CNN. We end by providing some practical recommendations on how to evaluate and diagnose the performance of a CNN. The goal of this section is to provide a first overview of the practicalities of building and fine-tuning a CNN for image classification. In Section 7 we show how to actually fine-tune a CNN using examples of interest to social scientists.

4.1 Fine-Tuning a CNN

CNNs with high predictive accuracy typically have many layers and are trained using hundreds of thousands (or even millions) of images. One of the more popular training sets, ImageNet, includes 1.3 million high-resolution images labeled for 1,000 different objects (such as different kinds of animals and vehicles). Recent CNNs trained on ImageNet have tens or even hundreds of layers. For example, the latest version of the CNN commonly known as ResNet has 152 layers (He, Zhang, et al. 2015).

Powerful computers with multiple graphics processing units (GPUs) are required to train such models. However, training CNNs from scratch is often unnecessary. Table 4.1 lists a substantial number of pretrained CNNs available through PyTorch's torchvision,[13] an open-source machine learning library for Python. The two right-hand columns of Table 4.1 report how well each CNN performed in predicting the 1,000 ImageNet labels. AlexNet (the first well-known CNN for image recognition), for example, incorrectly predicted the true label as its first guess 43.45% of the time. About one-fifth of the time (20.91%), none of its top five predictions were correct. Resnet-152, on the other hand, was much more accurate (21.69% Top-1 error and 5.94% Top-5 error).

Although each of these CNNs were originally trained to predict the 1,000 ImageNet classes, they can be adapted to perform new classification tasks (such as a binary prediction of whether or not an image includes people protesting). Fine-tuning takes advantage of the fact that a trained CNN has already "learned" a lot about which image features and parameter combinations perform best in predicting an image classification scheme. At a minimum, all that is required for fine-tuning is to alter the last fully connected layer of the network and do some minor retraining of parameters. As we will show in Section 7, high predictive accuracy is possible with fine-tuning, even with small training sets. Compared to training from scratch, the process also takes much less training time.

---

[13] https://pytorch.org/docs/stable/torchvision/models.html, last accessed April 26, 2020 (*torchvision.models — PyTorch Master Documentation* 2020).

Table 4.1 Pretrained CNNs available through PyTorch with error on
ImageNet

Network	Top-1 Error	Top-5 Error
AlexNet	43.45	20.91
VGG-11	30.98	11.37
VGG-13	30.07	10.75
VGG-16	28.41	9.62
VGG-19	27.62	9.12
VGG-11 with batch normalization	29.62	10.19
VGG-13 with batch normalization	28.45	9.63
VGG-16 with batch normalization	26.63	8.50
VGG-19 with batch normalization	25.76	8.15
ResNet-18	30.24	10.92
ResNet-34	26.70	8.58
ResNet-50	23.85	7.13
ResNet-101	22.63	6.44
ResNet-152	21.69	5.94
SqueezeNet 1.0	41.90	19.58
SqueezeNet 1.1	41.81	19.38
Densenet-121	25.35	7.83
Densenet-169	24.00	7.00
Densenet-201	22.80	6.43
Densenet-161	22.35	6.20
Inception v3	22.55	6.44

In our examples in Section 7, we fine-tune a pretrained 18-layer CNN from He, Zhang, et al. (2015) called ResNet (the "Res" stands for *residual learning*) eight times to build seven binary image classifiers and one multiclass image classifier. Figure 4.1 compares the architecture of 5 different ResNets. All of them start with a convolutional layer that includes 64 7×7 filters (conv1) followed by a max-pooling step. All of them also contain the same 4 convolutional "blocks" (conv2_x, conv3_x, conv4_x, and conv5_x). However, each has a different number of layers in each block. Compared to the others, ResNet-18 has fewer (4) layers in each of the 4 blocks (4 layers times 4 blocks plus the first convolutional layer and the last fully connected layer equals the total of 18 layers).

The main step for fine-tuning a pretrained CNN is to alter the last fully connected layer to predict the desired number of outcome classes. More complicated fine-tuning examples may also take additional steps, such as adding

layer name	output size	18-layer	34-layer	50-layer	101-layer	152-layer
conv1	112×112			7×7, 64, stride 2		
				3×3 max pool, stride 2		
conv2_x	56×56	$\begin{bmatrix} 3\times3,\ 64 \\ 3\times3,\ 64 \end{bmatrix}\times2$	$\begin{bmatrix} 3\times3,\ 64 \\ 3\times3,\ 64 \end{bmatrix}\times3$	$\begin{bmatrix} 1\times1,\ 64 \\ 3\times3,\ 64 \\ 1\times1,\ 256 \end{bmatrix}\times3$	$\begin{bmatrix} 1\times1,\ 64 \\ 3\times3,\ 64 \\ 1\times1,\ 256 \end{bmatrix}\times3$	$\begin{bmatrix} 1\times1,\ 64 \\ 3\times3,\ 64 \\ 1\times1,\ 256 \end{bmatrix}\times3$
conv3_x	28×28	$\begin{bmatrix} 3\times3,\ 128 \\ 3\times3,\ 128 \end{bmatrix}\times2$	$\begin{bmatrix} 3\times3,\ 128 \\ 3\times3,\ 128 \end{bmatrix}\times4$	$\begin{bmatrix} 1\times1,\ 128 \\ 3\times3,\ 128 \\ 1\times1,\ 512 \end{bmatrix}\times4$	$\begin{bmatrix} 1\times1,\ 128 \\ 3\times3,\ 128 \\ 1\times1,\ 512 \end{bmatrix}\times4$	$\begin{bmatrix} 1\times1,\ 128 \\ 3\times3,\ 128 \\ 1\times1,\ 512 \end{bmatrix}\times8$
conv4_x	14×14	$\begin{bmatrix} 3\times3,\ 256 \\ 3\times3,\ 256 \end{bmatrix}\times2$	$\begin{bmatrix} 3\times3,\ 256 \\ 3\times3,\ 256 \end{bmatrix}\times6$	$\begin{bmatrix} 1\times1,\ 256 \\ 3\times3,\ 256 \\ 1\times1,\ 1024 \end{bmatrix}\times6$	$\begin{bmatrix} 1\times1,\ 256 \\ 3\times3,\ 256 \\ 1\times1,\ 1024 \end{bmatrix}\times23$	$\begin{bmatrix} 1\times1,\ 256 \\ 3\times3,\ 256 \\ 1\times1,\ 1024 \end{bmatrix}\times36$
conv5_x	7×7	$\begin{bmatrix} 3\times3,\ 512 \\ 3\times3,\ 512 \end{bmatrix}\times2$	$\begin{bmatrix} 3\times3,\ 512 \\ 3\times3,\ 512 \end{bmatrix}\times3$	$\begin{bmatrix} 1\times1,\ 512 \\ 3\times3,\ 512 \\ 1\times1,\ 2048 \end{bmatrix}\times3$	$\begin{bmatrix} 1\times1,\ 512 \\ 3\times3,\ 512 \\ 1\times1,\ 2048 \end{bmatrix}\times3$	$\begin{bmatrix} 1\times1,\ 512 \\ 3\times3,\ 512 \\ 1\times1,\ 2048 \end{bmatrix}\times3$
	1×1			average pool, 1000-d fc, softmax		
FLOPs		1.8×10^9	3.6×10^9	3.8×10^9	7.6×10^9	11.3×10^9

Figure 4.1 Architecture of the convolutional neural nets trained by He, Zhang, et al. 2015, collectively known as ResNets.

layers or "freezing" some of the initial layers so that they are not adjusted with the addition of new data and training. ResNet-18 was originally developed to predict the 1,000 classes of the ImageNet competition corpus. For our examples in Section 7, we are primarily interested in predicting whether an image belongs to a single class or not (a binary classifier). In Figure 4.1 (in red), the last fully connected layer of ResNet-18 is a vector of 1,000 weights that is multiplied by the entire volume output from conv5_x (after first using average pooling to reduce the size of the output). A softmax (multinomial) model is then used to "translate" the resulting vector output into 1,000 class probabilities that add up to 1. For binary fine-tuning, we replace this last layer with a new $1 \times 1 \times 2$ fully connected layer. The starting weights of this $1 \times 1 \times 2$ layer are initialized at random (from a Gaussian distribution with a standard deviation of 0.01). After altering the architecture, we retrain the model for a set number of epochs using train and validation images that we know are true positives and true negatives for the classes of interest. For our examples in Section 7, we will generally set the train/validation split to 80%/20% (see Section 4.4 for more on this choice). In order to retrain the model with new images, we usually need to do some image preprocessing, as described in the next section.

4.2 Preprocessing

How do we go from having a set of image files on our computer to feeding them to a CNN while making sure they are appropriately formatted for accurate CNN training? There are three main objectives driving images preprocessing: (1) all of the images need to be of the same size, (2) the color intensities of the images should be normalized, and (3) we can consider increasing the size of the train set with data augmentation. The size of the input volume (images) needs to be constant because it determines the size of the intermediate layers and the size of some parameter matrices (e.g., the size of fully connected layers), which needs to be fixed. For example, input images need to be 224×224 pixels to fit into the ResNet architecture. We also want to normalize the input values (pixel-level color intensities ranging from 0 to 255) and center the mean of the color intensities around 0 because it facilitates calculating the gradient and the training of the CNN. Finally, we can artificially augment the size of our training sets (improving accuracy) by flipping or rotating images (and performing other tricks) during preprocessing.

4.2.1 Resizing

Figure 4.2 shows the four main operations that are (or can be) involved in preprocessing images to make sure they are all of the same size: squishing, cropping, rescaling, and padding. The example image in Figure 4.2 is taken from a dataset of images shared on Twitter in support of the #FamiliesBelong-Together movement (www.familiesbelongtogether.org/, last accessed April 26, 2020) in 2018. Users shared a wide range of images in support of the movement, including images of people wearing a jacket (or versions thereof) that Melania Trump wore on a visit to a shelter for immigrant children near the border with Mexico (see Cillizza [2018] for context). If we wanted to know where this coat appears in tens of thousands of images shared on Twitter, perhaps to test a theory of symbolic resonance in protest movements, we could fine-tune an existing classifier to recognize the coat. To do so, our training data of true positives and negatives must fit the input requirements of the CNN we are fine-tuning. Most existing open-source CNNs take inputs of a square size (images

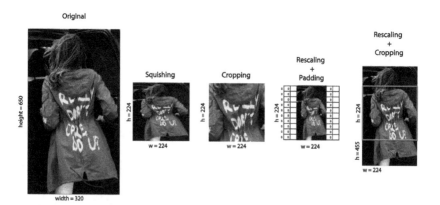

Figure 4.2 Image-resizing techniques.

with the same height and width), for example images of size 224 × 224 pixels. We have multiple options for how to resize images into this required size.

Squishing means resizing the original dimensions of an image to a particular size without keeping the image aspect ratio (the ratio between the height and width of the original picture). As you can see in Figure 4.2, if some images in your dataset are far from having square dimensions, this means that you need to substantially deform them, which is far from ideal because image and shape deformations can make it harder for the algorithm to learn how to classify particular classes/objects.

An alternative resizing approach is *cropping*: to use only part of the image (a *patch*) that fits the desired size. As you can see in Figure 4.2, in this case we are not deforming the image. However, given the big difference between height and width, we are only taking a small part of the picture into account. If, for example, the research objective is to find instances of images with people wearing the jacket, not including the jacket's arms and hood in the patch during training may lower the accuracy of the CNN.

Another option is *rescaling* the image, as shown in the two right subfigures in Figure 4.2. Rescaling consists of reducing the size of the image while maintaining its aspect ratio by decreasing the height or the width to the desired size (e.g., 224), and then decreasing the size of the other dimension such that we keep the same original proportion between height and width. This resizing technique avoids deforming the image. However, for nonsquare images, an extra step is needed to make sure the image fulfills the required square dimensions of most pretrained CNNs. One option is to use *padding*. This technique consists of adding as many columns (or rows) of 0s to the sides (or to the top or bottom) of the rescaled image as needed to fulfill the required input size (see second subfigure from the right in Figure 4.2). Padding might not be the best resizing approach if instances of the same class of interest in our dataset (e.g., images of people wearing versions of Melania Trump's jacket) have varied aspect ratios (e.g., some are of a vertical layout while others are more horizontal), and so for some instances we are padding the sides and for some others the top or bottom of the image. In this case a more suitable approach is to crop the images after rescaling (see the rightmost subfigure in Figure 4.2). Trying out different preprocessing choices can help improve the accuracy of the CNN.

4.2.2 Normalization

Two input *normalization* preprocessing steps can improve model accuracy as well as computation speed: scaling and centering. As we discussed in the previous section, images can be represented as three dimensional matrices (one dimension for each RGB color channel: red, green, and blue) where each cell indicates the intensity of that color in that particular pixel. The values indicating these color intensities usually range from 0 to 255. Two main problems emerge when using these original 0–255 values as inputs to train or fine-tune a CNN. First, two instances of the same class (e.g., two jacket images) might have different color intensities because one might be brighter than the other, making it difficult for the CNN to learn that those are indeed two examples of the same class. *Scaling* helps solve this problem by transforming all the data onto the same scale. Computer vision scholars often transform the raw pixel level intensities of an image into a standardized 0–1 range by applying Equation 4.1 (or a variant thereof) to each image pixel $x_{i,j}$ from each color channel z. On top of scaling, *centering* the values around 0 also helps with the calculation of the gradient, speeding up the learning process. For this reason, as indicated in Equation 4.2, practitioners often also subtract from each scaled pixel intensity y_{ijz} the mean of the intensities for that color (μ_z) and divide it by the standard deviation of the intensities (σ_z).

$$y_{ijz} = \frac{x_{ijz} - \frac{\sum_1^n x_{ijz}}{n}}{max(x_{ijz}) - min(x_{ijz})} \tag{4.1}$$

$$s_{ijz} = \frac{y_{ijz} - \mu_z}{\sigma_z} \tag{4.2}$$

4.2.3 Data Augmentation

One can artificially increase the size of a training set to improve the accuracy of a classifier by using different versions of the original images during training (Taylor and Nitschke 2017). Two main data augmentation techniques are often used: random crop and horizontal flip. As shown in Figure 4.3, *random crop* means selecting a different patch of a given image at each training epoch. As instances of the same class are likely to have different aspect ratios, this technique can improve the generalizability and accuracy of the CNN. Another way of increasing the number of training examples is by performing a *horizontal flip* (as shown in the rightmost subfigure in Figure 4.3). Usually, in each epoch researchers flip each picture in the training set based on a predetermined probability.

4.3 Preprocessing with Python

Python packages for deep learning programming come with off-the-shelf functions to apply the discussed preprocessing techniques. Code chunk 1 illustrates pytorch code for resizing, normalizing, and augmenting the training and validation data to be used for training or fine-tuning a CNN. The code assumes that a set of .jpg/.jpeg pictures are located in a particular data_path (see line 16), and that they have already been split into *train* and *validation* sets, and that the images belonging to each set have already been placed into two different subdirectories named *train* and *val*. The data_transforms object contains instructions about how to preprocess the training and validation images. In this case, before each forward propagation of the CNN we perform the following preprocessing to the images in the training set: (a) we crop a random 224×224 patch from the image (transforms.RandomResizedCrop(224); the patch will be different at each epoch), (b) we decide whether to flip the image (RandomHorizontalFlip(), with a default probability of .5), (c) we scale the pixel-level intensities to a 0–1 range (transforms.ToTensor()), and (d) we center scaled pixel- level instensities around 0, by taking into account the average and standard deviation of the intensities of the images in the training set for each color channel (transforms.Normalize()).

Then, for each image in the validation set: (a) we first rescale the image (transforms.Resize(256)), (b) we select the middle 224×224 patch, (c) we scale (transforms.ToTensor()) and (d) we center (transforms.Normalize()) the pixel level intensities (using the mean and standard deviations for each color channel based only on the images in the training set). Finally, the torch.utils.data.DataLoader() (lines 19 and 20) function takes care of loading the data in batches and applying these preprocessing steps at each epoch.

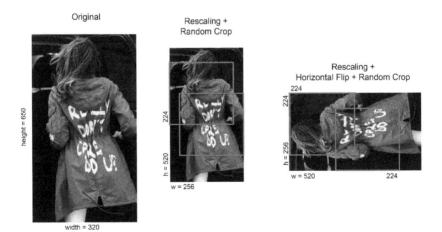

Figure 4.3 Data augmentation techniques.

```
1  from torchvision import transforms
2
3  data_transforms = {
4      'train': transforms.Compose([
5          transforms.RandomResizedCrop(224),
6          transforms.RandomHorizontalFlip(),
7          transforms.ToTensor(),
8          transforms.Normalize([0.485, 0.456, 0.406], [0.229, 0.224, 0.225])
9      ]),
10     'val': transforms.Compose([
11         transforms.Resize(256),
12         transforms.CenterCrop(224),
13         transforms.ToTensor(),
14         transforms.Normalize([0.485, 0.456, 0.406], [0.229, 0.224, 0.225])
15     ]),
16 }
17
18 data_dir = 'data_path/'
19 image_datasets = {x: datasets.ImageFolder(os.path.join(data_dir, x),
20                     data_transforms[x]) for x in ['train', 'val']}
21 dataloaders = {x: torch.utils.data.DataLoader(image_datasets[x],
22                     batch_size=4, shuffle=True, num_workers=4) for x in
23                     ['train', 'val']}
```

Listing 1 Pytorch code for image preprocessing

4.4 Hyperparameters in CNNs

Hyperparameters are elements of the model that the researcher specifies values for before fine-tuning begins (whereas the parameters of a model are updated during the training). We can think of them as tuning knobs, or as a set of dials that can be spun to different values. Researchers generally try many different combinations of hyperparameters over many rounds of fine-tuning, usually using a grid search of hyperparameters. The best hyperparameter configuration is the one that gives us the most accurate results in the shortest amount of time without overfitting. *Overfitting* means that the model has learned how to classify the images in the train set extremely well, but performs poorly on the the validation images. In short, the CNN does not generalize well to pictures outside the training set. For example, the model may produce an extremely accurate classifier of the Melania Trump jacket based on the training data. But if every image of the jacket in the training set is worn by a woman with dark hair, it may be that the model is overfitting by assigning a correct prediction based on the hair color, not on the jacket features. If this is the case, the trained model will fail on a picture of the jacket worn by someone with blonde or blue hair.

Unfortunately, the best combination of hyperparameters is not something that a researcher can know in advance. Figure 4.4 visualizes the predictive accuracy of different combinations of two parameters x and z (recall that state-of-the-art CNNs have millions of parameters). The peaks (in red) indicate better performing combinations (they have the lowest error rates). The best-performing combination, the global maximum (B), is located around ($x = 7$, $z = 1$). With millions of parameters, comparing every possible combination of parameters to find the global maximum would take a very long time. Hyperparameter settings typically specify how to constrain the parameter-space search in the interests of saving time and computing power. But in doing so these settings also introduce the possibility that we will not locate a highly accurate maximum, perhaps getting stuck on a less-accurate local maximum (A) instead. Figure 4.4 helps to explain why. Suppose that we considered only a limited range of x and z values in the interest of computational time. If we set a small number of model epochs (say, 10) and specify small jumps in values of x and z, then our search may never get to the combination of x and z that produces the best maximum, even if the model is exploring in the right direction. The model does not get to explore much of the parameter space with only 10 small jumps. On the other hand, if we specify large jumps, then we may skip over the best maximum entirely. Unfortunately, there is no way to know if we are at the best possible maximum. All we can do is try to get closer to it by experimenting with hyperparameter values (adjusting the size of the jump, or the *learning rate*, at each epoch in this toy example).

In the glossary below we describe the most important hyperparameters involved in training a CNN. In the example applications and code in Section 7, we try out a range of different hyperparameters to fine-tune a CNN classifier and explore the extent to which results depend on the specified setup. An excellent interactive (high-level) introduction to hyperparameters is available on the TensorFlow website.[14] Smith (2018) offers additional insights and tips for the "black art" of hyperparameter selection. Tanksale (2018) is also a nice introduction. Hyperparameter values can have an effect on the accuracy of the CNN. However, it is difficult to know *ex ante* which hyperparameters are more important in determining the accuracy of the model. Different tasks may require different tweaks to hyperparameters. Researchers usually try out different hyperparameter combinations to find out the one yielding the most accurate results (Domhan, Springenberg, and Hutter 2015). We build on our own experience to sort the following hyperparameter glossary based on relevance. We start with the hyperparameters that have had a large impact on the accuracy of

---

[14] https://playground.tensorflow.org, last accessed April 26, 2020 (*A Neural Network Playground* 2020).

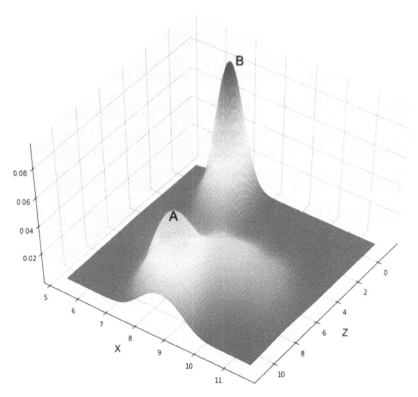

Figure 4.4 A nonconvex two-parameter space.

CNNs in our own research. We then transition to additional hyperparameters that can potentially affect accuracy.

- **Epochs/iterations:** Epochs are the number of times the model will train over the *full* set of images in the training set. Iterations are the number of forward propagations that it takes to complete an epoch. The number of iterations depends on the batch size (see definition of *batch size* below). If, for example, we split a dataset of 5,000 training images into batches of 500, it will take 10 iterations to complete an epoch. Usually one only executes backward propagation (and calculates the gradient) at the end of each epoch, after finishing all of the iterations and calculating the final loss for a given epoch. More epochs can lead to better results, but too many epochs can lead to model overfitting. Having a validation set (see *ratio of train-validation* below) can help prevent overfitting. CNN performance based on the training set tends to improve after each epoch. However, there usually comes a point after which each additional epoch results in worse accuracy based on the validation set. At that point we want to stop the training process because more epochs will likely result in a model that does not generalize well to new pictures. The number of epochs determines whether a model has been trained long enough (or for too long), and so it has a strong impact on the accuracy of the CNN. Researchers need to make a decision about the number of epochs both when training a CNN from scratch and when fine-tuning an existing model.

- **Learning rate:** How much the weights/coefficients can change in each model optimization (at the end of each epoch). We can think of this as how big a step we want the model to take in the potential coefficient space while it looks for the weights that minimize the error. If the step is too big, we will miss many potential weights combinations that could significantly reduce the error. If the step is too small, the model will take an extremely long time and may never reach potential weights combinations that minimize the error. Getting the "right" learning rate for a given model is generally approached with trial and error. Starting with a large rate and then decreasing it as the number of epochs increases is a common practice. The *step size* and *gamma* hyperparameters described below help to achieve this change in the learning rate as the number of epochs increases. You can modify the learning rate both when training a CNN from scratch as well as when fine-tuning a pretrained model.

- **Dropout rate:** A common practice to avoid overfitting (to avoid the model getting good at predicting the outcome for the images in the train but not the validation set) is to randomly set some of the values in the weight matrices and filters to 0. The dropout rate specifies how often we do so, expressed as the probability of setting a given weight to 0, usually set between 0.4 and 0.9 (Srivastava et al. 2014). See Budhiraja (2016) for more detail. When fine-tuning a pretrained model, one can decide to set a dropout rate for newly added layers as well as for pretrained layers (if one decides to allow the weights of pretrained layers to be updated).

- **Batch size:** When training or fine-tuning a CNN, in each epoch we want to use all images in the training set to make sure we take advantage of, and learn from, all available examples. However, there are two main reasons for not using them all at once when performing the forward and backward propagation and to instead pass them through the CNN in smaller batch sizes: (1) it helps reducing computation time and required memory and (2) it avoids model overfitting (Wilson and Martinez [2003], but only if we update the model weights [perform the backward propagation] after each iteration instead of at the end of each epoch). You can set the batch size both when training a CNN from scratch and when fine-tuning a pretrained one.

- **Ratio of train-validation:** The percentage split of labeled images, true positives and true negatives, into the train and validation sets. In each training epoch/iteration, the parameters in a CNN are learned via forward and backward propagation on the images in the train set. To prevent overfitting, the loss and accuracy of the CNN is measured by evaluating the difference between the class scores and the actual classes of the images in the validation set. In the examples we run in Section 7, we use an 80%-20% split, which is fairly standard in the field. Increasingly, researchers are using a train-validation-*test* split, along the lines of 80%-10%-10%, where a final chunk of images are used only for a final held-out check once the CNN has been trained under the preferred hyperparameter combination. Although images in the validation set are not used for training (as discussed earlier in the *Epochs/iterations* description), model performance on the validation set is often used to decide when to stop training the model over further iterations. Generally, researchers stop training when the loss for the validation set stops improving (even if the loss for the training set continues to improve). This could mean that we are indirectly overfitting/underfitting the model to the validation set (e.g., the validation loss for a different set might stop improving slightly sooner or slightly later). To assess the extent to which this is the case, once the CNN is trained, researchers check the out-of-sample accuracy one final time using a completely untouched *test* set that has not been used either for training or to decide when to stop training the CNN.

- **Loss function:** This determines how we evaluate the accuracy of the model. In a linear model, for example, we usually use the sum of squared errors as the loss function. The aim is to minimize the predictive loss (or error).

- **Activation functions:** ReLu, sigmoid, tanh, and other nonlinear transformations are applied to the data in different layers, as introduced in Figure 3.3 and seen in Figures 3.4(2) and 3.4(5). Unless you are developing a CNN from scratch, these are normally already set in the model that you are fine-tuning.

- **Optimizer:** This sets how we try to minimize the loss function (and maximize predictive accuracy) by slightly changing the model parameters and checking which configuration achieves the lowest error. Here we are deciding how to set the next weights configuration during back propagation. A common optimizer is Stochastic Gradient Descent (SGD), and SGD with momentum (see below for a description of *momentum*), but other optimizers are available and can be easily implemented using existing machine learning Python libraries. See Ruder (2016) for an overview on optimizers.

- **Momentum (or momentum factor):** The momentum and the learning rate in combination determine the "direction" (within a coefficient space) and size of the change in weights. Momentum helps prevent the model from becoming "stuck" by taking into consideration several of the previous gradients instead of exploring a specific direction of the parameter space based on a single gradient. This hyperparameter ranges from 0 to 1. Goh (2017) is a helpful post with more details.

- **Step size:** The step size and the gamma combine to shrink the learning rate as the number of epochs progresses. The step size defines after how long the learning rate is subject to decay. This will become relevant only if you have specified a number of epochs higher than the step size. For example, if the step size is 5 and the number of epochs is 20, after every five epochs the learning rate will shrink. Confusingly, some sources refer to the learning rate as the step size.
- **Gamma:** Decay (multiplicative) of the learning rate that will apply after every step-size number of epochs. Default in PyTorch is 0.1.

4.5 Diagnostics

How do we know if a trained model is performing well? To evaluate predictive performance, we use a standard set of measures. *Accuracy* refers to the proportion of cases (positive and negative) that are correctly predicted by the trained model. *Precision* refers to how often the predicted positive cases are correct, while *recall* refers to how often actual positive cases are predicted to be positive. An *F1* score is the harmonic mean of precision and recall. Put another way, precision is a measure of false positive error while recall is a measure of false negative error. The precision/recall distinction can be important because it provides additional information into the distribution of prediction errors. Depending on the objective, for example, a researcher may be more concerned with maximizing recall (to ensure that possible cases are not missed) than overall accuracy. A *confusion matrix* is a useful way to get a sense of how prediction errors are distributed (see Section 6 for examples).

To prevent overfitting, researchers check for model performance on a validation set that was not used for training. If over many epochs the training loss continues to drop while loss on the validation set flattens or increases, this is a sign of overfitting.

If a model is not performing as desired, researchers can adjust hyperparameters and train again. One of the advantages of images research, however, is that we can also easily look at the images that the model gets wrong. Is there something similar about the images that are false positives or false negatives? For example, do we see that all the false negatives for Melania Trump's jacket are worn by blondes? That may tell us that we need to include more diversity in the training images for the jacket. Adding more or more diverse training data may be a solution to poor model performance.

One of the challenges of evaluating where and how a CNN fails or succeeds is in the lack of interpretability of parameters or filters. It can be very difficult to tell which aspect of an image is driving classification, and if the model is picking up on some incidental feature instead of something that consistently drives classification, these models may have low generalizability. Ribeiro, Singh, and Guestrin (2016), for example, found that a model predicting whether a picture was of a husky or a wolf was being driven not by any features of the animals but instead by whether or not there was snow in the picture. Making the deep, abstract representations from hidden layers more interpretable by humans is a growing area of computer vision research, so we may be close to unlocking the deep learning black box (see Zhang and Zhu [2018] for an overview of current strategies for interpretability).

We return to diagnostics and specific techniques for improving model predictions in Section 7. Moving from the theory of deep learning and fine-tuning to applications, in the next section we introduce the original Black Lives Matter images study and describe the data provided for the applied examples.

5 Political Science Working Example: Images Related to a Black Lives Matter Protest

Having explained the theory and practicalities of working with CNNs for image classification, in Sections 6 and 7 we illustrate (1) how to use off-the-shelf autotaggers and (2) how to fine-tune your own CNN for addressing research questions of relevance to social scientists. In this section we introduce and contextualize the image dataset from our own prior research that we will use in these proceeding sections. In an earlier project (Casas and Webb Williams 2018), we studied whether the images included in social media posts could predict online social movement participation. Scholars believe that images play key roles in social movement participation in the digital media age (Bennett and Segerberg 2013; Bimber, Flanagin, and Stohl 2005; Castells 2012; Howard and Hussain 2013; Kharroub and Bas 2015). Systematic, large-N studies are rare, however. We wanted to study the impact of social media communications leading up to and during an offline protest. Could we test if the image content of a Twitter message predicted how likely it was that the message would be shared online?

For a two-week period around an April 14, 2015 Black Lives Matter protest (known as "Shutdown A14"), we collected Twitter messages containing one or more of the following keywords and hashtags: #shutdownA14, murder by police, mass incarceration, shutdownA14, killer cops, police murder, #A14, stop business as usual, stolenlives, massincarceration, stolen lives, #policebrutality, #stolenlives, #blacklivesmatter, and black lives. In total, we collected about 150,000 tweets. The tweets included around 9,500 unique images.

We were particularly interested in testing the following expectations as to why images might play a mobilizing role. First, the core hypotheses concerned the emotional content evoked by the pictures. Building on a specific model from political psychology, the *Affective Intelligence* model (Marcus, Neuman, and MacKuen 2000), we expected that images evoking higher levels of anger, enthusiasm, and fear/anxiety would attract more online attention (e.g., would be shared by a larger number of Twitter users), whereas images evoking higher levels of sadness would have the opposite effect. We also explored the role of disgust but had no clear expectation about its effect. Beyond these emotions effects, we had two other expectations that we used as controls in the analyses. First, we theorized that images are in part mobilizing because they can increase one's expectations about the success of a movement. To control for such an effect, we examined instances where images contained protesting crowds, which we argued were signals of the movement's success. We also theorized that images are in part mobilizing because they can activate social collective identities. To control for this mechanism we labeled images for symbols of collective identity, such as flags or religious symbols. After completing the study, we became interested in the potential effect that the presence of celebrities or other opinion leaders might have on mobilization. Although we have not tested this mechanism systematically, it drives our focus in this Element on identifying John Legend in images.

In the original project we (together with undergraduates and Mechanical Turk workers) manually assigned multiple labels to the images. Testing which theoretical mechanisms were more or less mobilizing required labeling these images for the presence or absence of certain features, including whether or not the picture contained a protest and/or a symbol of collective identity, and how the image made the annotator feel.

See Casas and Webb Williams (2018) for a complete presentation and discussion of the research design and findings. In Figures 5.1 and 5.2 we present the key findings of the study. In Figure 5.1 we show that in line with our expectations, higher levels of evoked enthusiasm and anxiety/fear were positively correlated with higher rates of online attention (the overall number of retweets – left subfigure) and online diffusion (retweets by users who had not previously messaged about the protest – right subfigure). We were not able to corroborate our expectation about the effect of evoked anger, but we did partially corroborate the hypothesis that images evoking sadness would be associated with lower levels of protest diffusion. As for the two control mechanisms (protest and symbol), we found support for the claim that images are in part mobilizing

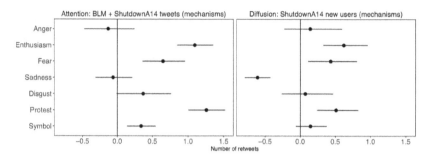

Figure 5.1 Figure 5 from Casas and Webb Williams (2018).

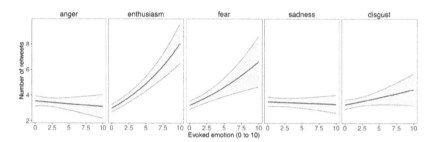

Figure 5.2 Figure 6 from Casas and Webb Williams (2018).

because they increase people's expectation about a movement's success and because they appeal to common social identities.

The findings are a good example of why social scientists should care about images and image effects. In addition, the images collected and labeled for that study serve as a real-world dataset for illustrating how to use CNNs for image classification. In the previous study we did not use the computer vision techniques introduced in this Element. But the study motivated our interest in computer vision, as we wondered whether or not we needed to invest so many resources in manual image labeling. We are currently working on a similar but much larger-scale project in which we develop and implement computer vision techniques to further study the role of images in protest mobilization – now that we have hundreds of thousands of images, automated techniques have become all the more appealing.

Here we pull subsets of the labeled image corpus to demonstrate how to use an off-the-shelf autotagging service (Amazon's Rekognition) and how to fine-tune an open-source CNN (from PyTorch). The full image corpus contains 8,148 unique images after image files smaller than 5kb are removed (small images usually do not provide sufficient learning data for CNNs). Each image has been labeled for whether it contained a protest, for whether it contained the singer John Legend (who appeared because of a statement he made against mass incarceration around the time of the protest), and for how much fear, anger, disgust, sadness, and enthusiasm the picture evoked in the annotator on a scale of 0 to 10. In other words, the emotion scale measures how viewers react to an image, *not* the emotions displayed by people in images.

Each of the 1,000 most commonly shared images in the corpus were labeled by multiple annotators. In these cases, we assign a positive score if *any* annotator indicated that an image contained a protest or John Legend. For the emotions labels, we used average scores. For example, if an image made the one annotator very angry (8 on a scale of 1–10) but had little effect on another (2 out of 10), then the anger score for the image would be averaged to 5.

In the next section on autotaggers, we draw on these gold standard labeled images to explore whether we could have successfully used a pretrained, off-the-shelf autotagger in our prior study. Then, in Section 7, we draw on these images to put fine-tuning a CNN to the test by performing the following specific tasks: (1) identifying images of protests, (2) identifying an opinion leader (the singer John Legend), and (3) capturing each of five emotions that an image may evoke in viewers.

6 The Promise and Limits of Autotaggers

By *off-the-shelf autotagger*, we mean pretrained algorithms that will generate image labels without any additional training. Many of these autotaggers rely on CNNs or variants thereof. While the main focus of this Element is on fine-tuning CNNs, autotaggers are an appealing means of processing large quantities of image data. Despite the limitations, we are aware that for many scholars, autotaggers are useful (see, for example, the commercial autotagging usage in Horiuchi, Komatsu, and Nakaya [2012] and Nanne et al. [2019]). We wish to bring both their benefits and their downsides to the attention of social scientists. However, researchers who know that autotaggers will not work for their research objectives may wish to skip this section and proceed to the fine-tuning examples.

Some autotaggers are available through commercial services such as Amazon's Rekognition, Microsoft's Computer Vision, or Google's Cloud Vision. Smaller companies, such as Clarifai, also exist and tend to specialize in particular types of commercial image labeling. These commercial services are relatively easy to use, will generate a long list of labels with probabilities for each image, and are free for smaller projects. They are also proprietary, meaning that researchers generally will not have access to the CNNs doing the labeling. There are also a number of open-source, noncommercial autotagger options made available by researchers such as Redmon and Farhadi (2018) and

Geitgey (2020). These open-source taggers may have a more limited set of labels that they have been trained to recognize, or they may only perform a single specific task, but it is possible for researchers to modify the taggers for their own proposes (as we do below by fine-tuning an open-source CNN).

These autotagging tools can be quite useful, especially for a researcher who is trying to get a general sense of what is in a large corpus of images by labeling for the presence of standard objects. ImageNet,[15] described in previous sections, is the benchmark dataset for many autotaggers (Russakovsky et al. 2015). A CNN trained on MS-Celeb-1M[16] will predict the faces of 100,000 identified celebrities (Guo et al. 2016). One trained on COCO[17] will locate 80 common objects within larger images (Lin et al. 2014).

Algorithms trained on these benchmark datasets can be powerful tools. By adding more labeled images, many autotaggers can now recognize far more than the original 1,000 ImageNet classes. Many autotaggers have also expanded far beyond the standard tasks of object detection and recognition. For example, Amazon's Rekognition service can pull text from an image; predict whether an image contains sensitive content; analyze faces (e.g., guess age, gender, and the emotion on the face); and recognize specific faces based on stored facial data specified by the user. Most of these API calls return both the result and a "confidence score" (the probability) for each image feature.

Despite their impressive strengths, these tools do have important limitations that, in our view, warrant an investment in learning how to fine-tune CNNs to perform custom tasks. One of the major limitations is that autotaggers many not include labels that are important to social scientists. In addition, the labels are not always accurate. Figure 6.1 presents Rekognition results for an image of a familiar scene from American politics – a television newsroom where an anchor and guest are discussing the White House. The Rekognition labels, however, seem to describe a very different scene – a meal at a diner or an excursion to the aquarium. Though explainable, these labels are also clearly wrong and unhelpful for a researcher trying to identify politically relevant images.

The labels provided for the sample image in Figure 6.2 seem more accurate though still imperfect (there is no highway in the image). The labels also fail to recognize the distinctive shape of the United States Capitol on the mug, much less the evocative repetition of that shape in the background.

---

[15] http://image-net.org/index, last accessed April 26, 2020 (*ImageNet* 2020).

[16] www.microsoft.com/en-us/research/project/ms-celeb-1m-challenge-recognizing-one-million-celebrities-real-world/, last accessed April 26, 2020 (*MS-Celeb-1M: Challenge of Recognizing One Million Celebrities in the Real World-Microsoft Research* 2020).

[17] http://cocodataset.org/#home, last accessed April 26, 2020 (*COCO – Common Objects in Context* 2020).

Figure 6.1 Rekognition labels with confidence: Human 99.1 Bar Counter 98.4 Pub 98.4 Diner 97.1 Food 97.1 Worker 83.4 Animal 76.4 Aquarium 76.4 Sea Life 76.4.

Source: https://twitter.com/AmericaNewsroom/status/910493241283358720

Figure 6.2 Rekognition labels with confidence: Coffee Cup 98.2 Cup 98.2 Road 60.6 Freeway 52.6 Highway 52.6 Building 50.5 City 50.5 Downtown 50.5

Source: https://twitter.com/SteveDaines/status/910494836729483264

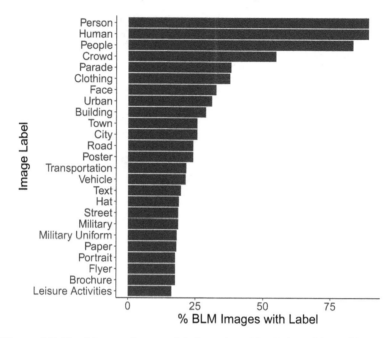

Figure 6.3 Top 25 most frequent labels assigned by Rekognition with >50% confidence

We tested a sample of 815 images from our Black Lives Matter corpus using Rekognition. Figure 6.3 reports the twenty-five most commonly returned labels. Based on these labels, we might conclude that there are no images of protest in the corpus. In fact, we know that there are many protest images in the corpus, but Rekognition does not include a protest category. Autotaggers are only as good as their training data and the labels they were assigned to learn. Problematically, especially in the case of commercial autotaggers, researchers do not know what constitutes the universe of potential labels. Only by running the images through Rekognition did we learn that there was no protest tag (or at least no protest tag that was returned – it may be that Amazon has trained for that label but is suppressing results).

To further illustrate the point about the limitations of labels available from different commercial autotagging services, we ran the same 815 BLM images through two other commercial autotagging services – Google's Cloud Vision and Microsoft's Computer Vision. Figure 6.4 displays the top ten most frequently returned tags from each service for the images. Note that the distribution of labels is quite varied based on the service. Google's Cloud Vision does return an explicit "protest" tag, for example, and also a tag for "demonstration." Microsoft has a "group" tag that was used often for the BLM images but was

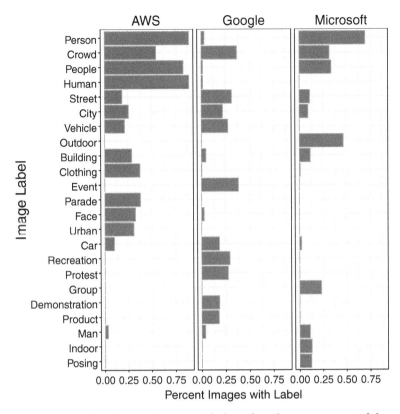

Figure 6.4 Top 10 most frequent labels assigned across commercial autotaggers

never returned by the other services. All three services returned a "crowd" tag, but at very different rates. These differing results should give researchers pause, and they speak to the need to carefully validate any autotagger results, whether commercial or open source, based on the required research task.

Algorithmic bias is a potential concern in any computer vision project and another reason to be careful when using autotaggers. Taggers are only as good as their training data, and recent discoveries have drawn attention to biases along dimensions of race and gender. Simonite (2017) points to sexism in image taggers, while Simonite (2018) notes racial bias (see also the useful discussion in Lam et al. [2019]). It is essential that researchers validate their results using a subset of "ground truth" images before using autotagger results in analyses.

Another concern for researchers is reproducibility. Commercial services may not share the details of their models and data (or their universe of labels as described earlier). It is difficult to know if the underlying model is even a

CNN. And the models and data may be constantly updated as users upload new images and as firms seek to improve accuracy by using that data for retraining. Replicating labels from these services may therefore prove challenging, as the underlying model may change between different passes of images through the autotagger. Some services, such as IBM's Visual Recognition, do offer version control, a potential solution to this issue.

Finally there are privacy concerns. Many of these services retain copies of submitted images and the predicted labels. How these images are used once uploaded is largely beyond a researcher's control. We discuss these ethical considerations in more detail in Section 8.

Open-source autotaggers may not be as sophisticated and easy to use as commercial services, but they can work quite well and help to address concerns about research reproducibility and data privacy. As discussed in Section 7, they also offer the possibility of fine-tuning, where a preexisting algorithm is trained to assign a new set of labels.

6.1 Using a Commercial Autotagger: Amazon's Rekognition

If a researcher is using a commercial autotagger in their project pipeline, once images are collected and a subset is labeled for validation purposes, the images are passed through the autotagger using an API. The results from the API calls are stored and compared to manual labels for validation. We next discuss the specific steps required to access one such service, Amazon's Rekognition. The general steps for using Amazon's Rekognition autotagger are:

1. Gather images.
2. Deduplicate images.
3. Manually label a subset of images to validate autotagger accuracy.
4. Generate a list of images to tag.
5. Create Amazon Web Services (AWS) account and securely save keys.
6. Decide which Rekognition API call to use.
7. Use boto3 package in Python to run images from the list through the API.
8. Save the API results.
9. Check results for accuracy using manual labels.
10. If accuracy is acceptable, label additional images with API. If not, invest in fine-tuning.

The specifics of the above steps will vary by commercial service (Amazon, Microsoft, Google, etc.) and across open-source autotaggers. We also do not address the first nontrivial task of collecting the images to be labeled. Deduplication reduces the number of images to be passed through the service (no need to pay twice for the same picture). The deduplication process will depend on the image source. For example, identical images from different tweets typically have the same URL, so the URL can be used to deduplicate. When there is no comparable metadata, the images themselves can be compared for similarity. An example deduplication script is available in the associated Github repo.[18] With the correct setup of paths and image format (noting that the script is written for jpgs), this script uses pixel similarity to build a CSV table linking the first unique instance of an image to every other identical image in a corpus. As always, it is important to visually confirm that the process is working as expected.

Autotaggers may not include a researcher's labels of interest. For autotagging services that do not publish a full list of possible tags, the only way to know if the service can accurately predict the desired label is compare the results to a set of prelabeled images. This makes it possible to numerically assess the autotagger's accuracy, precision, and recall.

A step-by-step guide to using the AWS Rekognition API is posted as a guide in the accompanying Github.[19] Creating an AWS account is simple,[20] and AWS also offers helpful instructions for setting up and securely saving access keys[21] once an account has been created. The next question is which of their services to use. For example, Rekognition offers many different API calls,[22] each of which returns different results or combinations of results.

In this example, we use two Rekognition API calls: "Detecting Objects and Scenes" and "Recognizing Celebrities." The Python code and sample images for these example applications are available in the project Github repo.[23] The code details how to loop images stored locally through the Rekognition API to detect labels[24] or to detect celebrities.[25] We also offer the same code in the

---

[18] https://github.com/norawebbwilliams/images_as_data/blob/master/code/03-image-deduplica tion.py, last accessed April 26, 2020 (Webb Williams and Casas 2020).

[19] https://github.com/norawebbwilliams/images_as_data/blob/master/notes/02-aws-rekognition-own-machine.md, last accessed April 26, 2020 (Webb Williams and Casas 2020).

[20] https://portal.aws.amazon.com/billing/signup#/start, last accessed April 26, 2020.

[21] https://aws.amazon.com/getting-started/, last accessed April 26, 2020.

[22] https://docs.aws.amazon.com/rekognition/latest/dg/what-is.html, last accessed April 26, 2020.

[23] https://github.com/norawebbwilliams/images_as_data, last accessed April 26, 2020 (Webb Williams and Casas 2020).

[24] https://github.com/norawebbwilliams/images_as_data/blob/master/code/AWS_rekognition/01 _aws_rekog_labels_example_py3.5.py, last accessed April 26, 2020 (Webb Williams and Casas 2020).

[25] https://github.com/norawebbwilliams/images_as_data/blob/master/code/AWS_rekognition/02 _aws_rekog_celeb_example_py3.5.py, last accessed April 26, 2020 (Webb Williams and Casas 2020).

form of Jupyter notebooks.[26] The same code and notebooks are available in the accompanying Code Ocean capusule, but note that this code will not run because there are no API keys included with the capsule. The Rekognition API response object (the result of an API call) contains many fields – for example, see this official Rekognition API documentation,[27] which lists everything that is returned for the "objects and scenes" API call.

The example code we provide extracts, organizes, and exports the returned fields of interest into a CSV file. Each row in the file includes an image-label (for object detection) or an image-celebrity-face (for celebrity recognition).

Rekognition offers a limited number of free API calls per year and account (at the time of writing it was 5,000). If you have already used your free credits, you will pay for each API call. For example, if you run the same image through both "Detecting Objects and Scenes" and "Recognizing Celebrities" you will be charged for two calls. For current pricing see the official AWS site.[28] Commercial services also typically offer discounts for educators. Amazon offers free credits for students and faculty through AWS Educate.[29]

6.2 Results from Amazon's Rekognition

We ran the 815 most frequently shared BLM images through the object recognition API to see whether Rekognition would identify street protests (according to our annotators, 422 out of the 815 images contained a protest). This experiment revealed that Rekognition does not appear to have a protest label, as that tag was never returned by the API for any of our images. It is also possible that it has been suppressed and is not publicly available, or perhaps the protest tag exists but is extremely inaccurate.

Rekognition did assign a "crowd" label to 446 of our images with at least 50% confidence. Most of our protest images did contain crowds of people, so as a validation example we compared the results of these two tags. The confusion matrix presented in Table 6.1 reports precision and recall. If we were to consider the "crowd" tag as an appropriate proxy for protest images, the overall accuracy of the autotagger would be 85.3%, with precision of 83.9% and recall of 88.6%. Rekognition produced more false positive errors (crowds that were not protests) than false negative errors (protests that were not labeled as crowds). This seems plausible given the lack of perfect congruity between a tag for protest and a

---

[26] https://github.com/norawebbwilliams/images_as_data/tree/master/notebooks/AWS_rekogni tion, last accessed April 26, 2020 (Webb Williams and Casas 2020).

[27] https://boto3.amazonaws.com/v1/documentation/api/latest/reference/services/rekognition.html #Rekognition.Client.detect_labels, last accessed April 26, 2020.

[28] https://aws.amazon.com/rekognition/pricing/, last accessed April 26, 2020.

[29] https://aws.amazon.com/education/awseducate/, last accessed April 26, 2020.

Table 6.1 Protest – Crowd Confusion Matrix (Number of images per category)

	No Protest (Manual)	Yes Protest (Manual)
No Crowd (AWS)	321	48
Yes Crowd (AWS)	72	374

Table 6.2 John Legend Confusion Matrix (Number of images per category)

	No Legend (Manual)	Yes Legend (Manual)
No Legend (AWS)	779	5
Yes Legend (AWS)	0	31

tag for a crowd. People often gather for reasons other than protests (concerts, for example), so there may be images in the corpus that Rekognition correctly identifies as crowds that are not actually protests. And protests do not always have to involve large crowds.

Despite the lack of an explicit "protest" tag, Rekognition might still be using a filtering step for a project that needed to identify images of street protests. After obtaining Rekognition results identifying crowds, a research team could manually exclude the ones that were not protests. This could save considerable time, although we would expect this would undercount protest images that did not include crowds.

We also ran the 815 most common BLM images through the celebrity detector. At least one of our annotators recognized John Legend in 36 of these images. Rekognition recognized him in 31 images. Table 6.2 reports overall accuracy at an impressive 99.4%. Every image that Rekognition labeled as John Legend was correct (100% precision). However, Rekognition missed 5 images of John Legend identified by our annotators (86.1% recall). If we intended to use Rekognition to label many more images for celebrities, we would want to better understand these errors. Perhaps the false negatives are more complicated images (e.g., they include multiple individuals)? Of course, it is also possible that the false negatives reveal errors in our "gold standard" manual labels and that Rekognition is actually more accurate than the initial results suggest.

Autotaggers can be very useful for exploring a large image corpus. They can automatically assign many labels along with confidence scores to each image. This wealth of information does not require manual labeling beyond what is needed for validation and may lead to interesting discoveries and hypothesis generation. We were surprised, for example, to discover that Rekognition detected additional celebrities in our BLM images, including Pharell Williams and Dr. Cornel West. Autotagger services may also generate useful labels of interest (despite failing in our case for protests). In these cases it is important to have a gold standard set of labels to assess accuracy. Even when an autotagger does not offer labels of interest, automatic and manual labeling may be combined in ways that reduce the costs of a labeling project (using autotaggers as a first-round filtering procedure, for example, to limit the amount of manual labeling required in a second round).

However, as noted above, there are issues with using autotaggers, and particularly with using commercial autotaggers, for image classification. An alternative that we turn to next is to fine-tune a pretrained open-source CNN algorithm. When fine-tuning, a researcher is no longer dependent on available autotagger labels and retains control over the images and results. In contrast to autotagging, the researcher must provide prelabeled images for training. But fine-tuning can often produce accurate results with a relatively small number of labeled examples.

7 Application: Fine-Tuning an Open-Source CNN

In this section, we demonstrate how to use fine-tuning to train seven binary CNN classifiers and one multiclass CNN classifier. The first example classifier performs an object recognition task – identifying street protests. The second is a facial recognition task – identifying images of John Legend. The rest of the binary tasks predict whether an image evokes each of five emotions – anger, disgust, enthusiasm, fear, and sadness. Finally, the multiclass classifier shows how to use the same method to predict an outcome that has more than two classes – the faces of six world leaders. In each case our goal is to illustrate the steps involved in fine-tuning a CNN.

Fine-tuning a CNN to label images for user-provided content categories entails the following steps:

1. Gather images.
2. Deduplicate images.
3. Preprocessing: standardize image pixel size, remove small images, etc. Additional preprocessing may occur later in pipeline depending on CNN selection and initial training results.
4. Manually label a subset of the images for the content of interest.
5. Split into train/validation sets (possibly adding supplemental images).
6. Select a pretrained CNN.

Table 7.1 Description of the Binary Computational Examples Data

CNN-classifier	Example	N	True Pos (train|validation)	True Neg (train|validation)
Protest	Ex. 1	199	99 (79|20)	100 (80|20)
John Legend	Ex. 2	199	99 (79|20)	100 (80|20)
Anger	Ex. 3	194	97 (77|20)	97 (77|20)
Disgust	Ex. 3	241	121 (96|24)	120 (96|25)
Enthusiasm	Ex. 3	1,468	734 (587|147)	734 (587|147)
Fear	Ex. 3	97	49 (38|10)	48 (39|10)
Sadness	Ex. 3	874	437 (349|88)	437 (349|88)

7. Adjust the last layer of the CNN for the number of classes.
8. Set initial hyperparameters.
9. Train the model and check accuracy using validation set.
10. Adjust hyperparameters or try different initial pretrained weights and retrain/validate.
11. When satisfied with accuracy, apply the trained model to unlabeled images.

In previous sections we describe how we gathered (step 1), deduplicated (step 2),[30] removed small images (step 3), and manually tagged our test BLM images (step 4). We now describe the research decisions we made to construct our train/validation sets for the seven binary classifiers. Table 7.1 summarizes the number of images used in the train/validation sets for each task. In some cases the corpus is relatively small (just 200 labeled images). This would be insufficient for training a CNN from scratch, but we show that it can be effective for fine-tuning an existing CNN when the task at hand is relatively simple. This is because pretrained deep neural nets have already learned important generic features of images.

In all of the examples we use *balanced* datasets, which means that we have the same number of true positives and true negatives. This will rarely be the case when training your own classifiers on real-world data: you are likely to have an uneven split of positive and negative cases in a corpus. Nevertheless, in these examples we use balanced datasets because it is much easier to discuss their accuracy: we know that a model classifying our images at random would get it right 50% of the time, meaning that we have an easy and intuitive baseline to

---

[30] For a sample deduplication script see: https://github.com/norawebbwilliams/images_as_data/blob/master/code/03-image-deduplication.py, last accessed April 26, 2020 (Webb Williams and Casas 2020).

judge the results. When dealing with unbalanced classes, training models with balanced datasets might help improve performance (Mountassir, Benbrahim Hourda, and Berrada 2012) but it does not necessarily need to be the case (Burns et al. 2011): trying both is advised. In all of the examples we use 80% of the true positives and true negatives for training and 20% for validation. The following sections describe the data used in each example in greater detail.

7.1 Data for Example 1: Predicting Images of Protests

We train this algorithm with 100 unique true positive and 99 unique true negative images of protests drawn from the full dataset of 8,148 images. The majority of the true positive images contained multiple people standing outside with signs, while the true negatives included a range of varied images from the corpus, including headshots and political cartoons. An example compilation image with four examples of true positives (top row) and four examples of true negatives (bottom row) is available here.[31] Alternatively, readers can view the training data in the accompanying Code Ocean capsule.[32]

7.2 Data for Example 2: Predicting Images of an Opinion Leader (John Legend)

To train a John Legend classifier, we used 28 unique positive images drawn from our BLM corpus and combined them with another 71 images of him from a Google image search. We then selected, as true negatives, similar images (headshots and pictures of a single person standing) from our BLM dataset (n = 50) and from the Internet (n = 50). For this example, we supplemented the BLM data with images from the Internet in order to have enough data to work with (28 true positive images is not much to learn from) and to train a more general facial recognition algorithm. The images of John Legend in the BLM data were almost exclusively headshots that pictured him alone against a clear backdrop. If those were our true positive images and all of the true negatives were of on-street protests, for example, the algorithm might learn to recognize headshots, as opposed to the specific facial features of John Legend. An example compilation image with four examples of true positives from the BLM dataset (first row), four examples of true negatives from the BLM dataset (second row), and four examples of true negatives selected from the Internet (third row, pictures of Don Cheadle, Rihanna, Leonardo DiCaprio, and Danny

---

[31] https://norawebbwilliams.github.io/ce_images/protest_examples.jpg, last accessed April 26, 2020.

[32] https://doi.org/10.24433/CO.2462313.v1, last accessed April 26, 2020 (Webb Williams, Casas, and Wilkerson 2020).

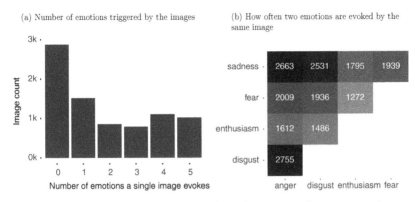

Figure 7.1 Images in our dataset often trigger more than one emotion

Glover) is available here.[33] Alternatively, readers can view the training data in the accompanying Code Ocean capsule.[34]

7.3 Data for Example 3: Predicting the Emotions Images Evoke in Viewers

Labeling images for evoked emotions (manually and automatically) is typically more difficult that labeling them for the presence of objects in large part because emotions are much more subjective. Another complication is that an image may trigger multiple emotional reactions. Our annotators found that about 35% of the BLM images did not trigger any emotion, while about 50% of the images evoked more than one emotion (see Figure 7.1a). Only about 19% of the images evoked a single emotion. Figure 7.1b shows how frequently an image that evoked a given emotion also evoked another emotion. For example, images triggering anger were also very likely to trigger feelings of sadness and disgust.

Prior research on visual sentiment analysis in computer science (e.g., Peng et al. 2015) recommends training with images that "clearly" trigger each emotion as the true positive cases. As a reminder, we originally had annotators rate each image on a 0–10 scale for each emotion. For this example, we use the average of those annotations to create binary labels in several steps. We first retain only images with a score of 3 or higher for a given emotion. We then further restrict the positive cases to emotionally distinct images by excluding those

---

[33] https://norawebbwilliams.github.io/ce_images/face_recognition_example.jpg, last accessed April 26, 2020.

[34] https://doi.org/10.24433/CO.2462313.v1, last accessed April 26, 2020 (Webb Williams, Casas, and Wilkerson 2020).

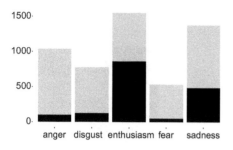

Emotion	Max Class	Clear Max
anger	935	97
disgust	648	121
enthusiasm	686	734
fear	484	49
sadness	889	437

Figure 7.2 Number of images that have each emotion as a max class (gray) or as a "clear" max class, meaning at least a 3-point difference with the 2nd highest emotion score (in black)

where the difference between the highest and second highest scoring emotions is less than 3. For the negative cases in the training data, we use images that scored 0 across all of the emotions. Thus the goal is to compare clear cases of a given emotion with cases that evoke no emotions at all. This should make it easier for a computer vision algorithm to learn the image features that are predictive of each emotion. The drawback is that this procedure significantly reduces the size of the training set from over 8,000 unique images to 97 true positives for anger, 121 for disgust, 734 for enthusiasm, 49 for fear, and 437 for sadness (see Figure 7.2). For each emotion we complement the positive training set with an equal number of randomly drawn images that evoked no emotion (true negatives). Asking an algorithm to predict the emotions that a wide variety of images evoke with such a small number of cases is a tall order. Given the relatively larger numbers of true positive images evoking enthusiasm and sadness, we would expect to achieve better accuracy for these emotions. Nevertheless, as we discuss in the results section, state-of-the-art CNNs might not be suited for addressing some complex questions of interest to social scientists (such as predicting evoked emotions).

7.4 Directory Structure and Code for Fine-Tuning

After collecting images and setting the train/validation split for the binary classifiers, we structure the images for each of the examples using the following directory structure.

- "train": contains the images used for training, with subdirectories for:
  - "negative": images that DON'T have the outcome we want to predict (e.g., do not have a protesting crowd, John Legend, or images evoking the emotion of interest)
  - "positive": images that DO have the outcome of interest

- "val": contains images used only to validate out of sample accuracy, with subdirectories for:
  - "negative": images that DON'T have the outcome we want to predict (e.g., do not have a protesting crowd, John Legend, or images evoking the emotion of interest)
  - "positive": images that DO have the outcome of interest

The directory structure distinguishes between the sample images that will be used for training and the ones that will be used for validation, as well as the true positives from the true negatives.

The data and the code to run these examples are available on two different platforms – Github and Code Ocean. On both platforms the file structure is the the the same. On Github, data and code are available in this repository.[35] The *data* directory contains a separate folder with the images for each of the classifier examples (protest, legend, anger, disgust, enthusiasm, fear, sadness, and world_leaders), as well as ACCURACY and MODELS folders to store information about the accuracy of each CNN after each epoch as well as the best performing model for each example.

The *notebooks* directory contains Jupyter Notebooks with the code for running the examples, one Notebook for running the binary classifiers (02_fine_tune_binary_models.ipynb) and another for running the multiclass example (03_fine_tune_multiclass_model.ipynb) (Webb Williams and Casas 2020). A functions script (00_functions.py) contains some helper functions for image preprocessing and other tasks. To run these notebooks on your own machine requires cloning the repository and having all of the software and hardware requirements installed. As discussed in Section 2, a better alternative is to use a virtual machine (cloud computer) with all of the dependencies already installed. We have made instructions available on how to use an AWS EC2 instance that will allow you to do this. You can find the instructions in the *notes* directory of the repository: 01-launch-use-ec2-aws-instances.md (Webb Williams and Casas 2020).

For those who are not familiar with AWS or who would rather not go through the process of setting up their own virtual instance, we have also made the code available on Code Ocean,[36] an online replication platform that will allow you to run the code for free (for up to 10 hours a month if you sign up with a educational .edu email account) on a virtual machine that already has everything

---

[35] https://github.com/norawebbwilliams/images_as_data, last accessed April 26, 2020 (Webb Williams and Casas 2020).

[36] https://doi.org/10.24433/CO.2462313.v1, last accessed April 26, 2020 (Webb Williams, Casas, and Wilkerson 2020).

needed installed. See Section 2 for information on how to take advantage of this option. The data, code, and directory structure are the same on either option.

In the Jupyter Notebooks we use a Python package (PyTorch) and our own helper functions to fine-tune an open-source CNN. PyTorch is one of many framework options for deep learning in Python. Other options include Tensorflow (developed by Google) and Keras. We use PyTorch for fine-tuning for several reasons. The "torchvision" module makes it easy to obtain and load pretrained CNNs. Table 4.1 (based on the official PyTorch documentation[37]) lists the large number of computer vision CNNs currently available with torchvision. Second, it is easy to edit the layers of pre-trained CNNs in PyTorch. This is essential for fine-tuning, where at a minimum the researcher needs to adjust the number of classes predicted in the final layer. Another longer-term consideration is that PyTorch is developed by Facebook. This means that it has a strong base of support and incentives for keeping up with the latest developments.

7.5 Binary Classification with Fine-Tuned ResNet-18 CNN

We fine-tune a pretrained CNN called ResNet-18 (He, Zhang, et al. 2015). As a reminder from Section 4, Figure 7.3 compares the architecture of 5 different ResNets. All of them start with a convolutional layer that includes 64 7×7 filters (conv1) followed by a max-pooling step. All of them also contain the same 4 convolutional "blocks" (conv2_x, conv3_x, conv4_x, and conv5_x). However, each has a different number of layers in each block.

layer name	output size	18-layer	34-layer	50-layer	101-layer	152-layer
conv1	112×112			7×7, 64, stride 2		
				3×3 max pool, stride 2		
conv2_x	56×56	$\begin{bmatrix} 3\times3,\,64 \\ 3\times3,\,64 \end{bmatrix}\times2$	$\begin{bmatrix} 3\times3,\,64 \\ 3\times3,\,64 \end{bmatrix}\times3$	$\begin{bmatrix} 1\times1,\,64 \\ 3\times3,\,64 \\ 1\times1,\,256 \end{bmatrix}\times3$	$\begin{bmatrix} 1\times1,\,64 \\ 3\times3,\,64 \\ 1\times1,\,256 \end{bmatrix}\times3$	$\begin{bmatrix} 1\times1,\,64 \\ 3\times3,\,64 \\ 1\times1,\,256 \end{bmatrix}\times3$
conv3_x	28×28	$\begin{bmatrix} 3\times3,\,128 \\ 3\times3,\,128 \end{bmatrix}\times2$	$\begin{bmatrix} 3\times3,\,128 \\ 3\times3,\,128 \end{bmatrix}\times4$	$\begin{bmatrix} 1\times1,\,128 \\ 3\times3,\,128 \\ 1\times1,\,512 \end{bmatrix}\times4$	$\begin{bmatrix} 1\times1,\,128 \\ 3\times3,\,128 \\ 1\times1,\,512 \end{bmatrix}\times4$	$\begin{bmatrix} 1\times1,\,128 \\ 3\times3,\,128 \\ 1\times1,\,512 \end{bmatrix}\times8$
conv4_x	14×14	$\begin{bmatrix} 3\times3,\,256 \\ 3\times3,\,256 \end{bmatrix}\times2$	$\begin{bmatrix} 3\times3,\,256 \\ 3\times3,\,256 \end{bmatrix}\times6$	$\begin{bmatrix} 1\times1,\,256 \\ 3\times3,\,256 \\ 1\times1,\,1024 \end{bmatrix}\times6$	$\begin{bmatrix} 1\times1,\,256 \\ 3\times3,\,256 \\ 1\times1,\,1024 \end{bmatrix}\times23$	$\begin{bmatrix} 1\times1,\,256 \\ 3\times3,\,256 \\ 1\times1,\,1024 \end{bmatrix}\times36$
conv5_x	7×7	$\begin{bmatrix} 3\times3,\,512 \\ 3\times3,\,512 \end{bmatrix}\times2$	$\begin{bmatrix} 3\times3,\,512 \\ 3\times3,\,512 \end{bmatrix}\times3$	$\begin{bmatrix} 1\times1,\,512 \\ 3\times3,\,512 \\ 1\times1,\,2048 \end{bmatrix}\times3$	$\begin{bmatrix} 1\times1,\,512 \\ 3\times3,\,512 \\ 1\times1,\,2048 \end{bmatrix}\times3$	$\begin{bmatrix} 1\times1,\,512 \\ 3\times3,\,512 \\ 1\times1,\,2048 \end{bmatrix}\times3$
	1×1			average pool, 1000-d fc, softmax		
FLOPs		1.8×10^9	3.6×10^9	3.8×10^9	7.6×10^9	11.3×10^9

Figure 7.3 Architecture of the Convolutional Neural Nets trained by He, Zhang, et al. 2015, collectively known as ResNets.

---

[37] https://pytorch.org/docs/stable/torchvision/models.html, last accessed April 26, 2020 (*torchvision.models — PyTorch Master Documentation* 2020).

As previously discussed, the main step for fine-tuning a pretrained CNN is to alter the last fully connected layer to predict the desired number of outcome classes. ResNet-18 was originally developed to predict the 1,000 classes of the ImageNet competition corpus. In our binary examples, we are only interested in predicting whether an image belongs to a single class or not. In Figure 7.3 (in red), the last fully connected layer is a vector of 1,000 weights. We replace this last layer with a new $1 \times 1 \times 2$ fully connected layer. The initial weights of this $1 \times 1 \times 2$ layer are randomly assigned from a Gaussian distribution with a standard deviation of 0.01. To use ResNet-18 we also take a few additional image preprocessing steps, mainly resizing all of our images to 224×224 pixels (ResNet's original input volume from ImageNet).

As discussed in Section 4, we experiment with many hyperparameter settings to see which combination garners the highest predictive accuracy. We fix two hyperparameters, the gamma (=0.01) suggested by the literature (Tai and Liu 2016), and a step size that allows us to reduce the learning rate several times during training (=7). We then experiment with different values for several other hyperparmeters (learning rate, momentum factor, and batch size). We draw on the results of these experiments to decide which hyperparameter settings to vary in our main tests. Importantly, the hyperparameter settings that work best for one classification task are not necessarily the best for another task.

To illustrate the impact of different learning rates (0.01, 0.001, and 0.0001), momentum factors (0.7 and 0.9), and image batch sizes (1, 4), we trained 12 versions of one of the binary classifiers (the model predicting images of John Legend) using 50 epochs. As a reminder, the learning rate specifies how much parameter values change as they are updated in each epoch (see Section 4.4 for more details). Larger learning rate values mean bigger "jumps" through the parameter space. Higher momentum factor values give more weight to previous gradient information, decreasing the likelihood of spending too long exploring suboptimal maximums. Finally, smaller image batch sizes decrease the likelihood of overfitting (but also increase the time required to train the model).

In Figure 7.4, *loss* represents the difference between the predicted and the actual class scores at each epoch (softer green-purple lines, values indicated in the left y-axis). *Accuracy* represents the proportion (or percentage) of correct model predictions (stronger green-purple lines, values indicated in the right y-axis). In the subfigures, loss and accuracy are averaged across batches to produce a single epoch score. Ideally, loss should decrease while accuracy increases as model fit improves with each epoch. We see that the model with a big jump learning rate (0.01) and a momentum factor giving more weight to recent gradient information (0.9) has the highest loss (0.17) and lowest

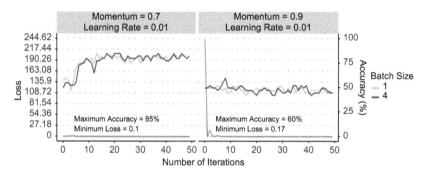

Figure 7.4 Hyperparameter Test: Trying different learning rates, momentum factors, and batch sizes. *Results for models with a 0.01 learning rate.*

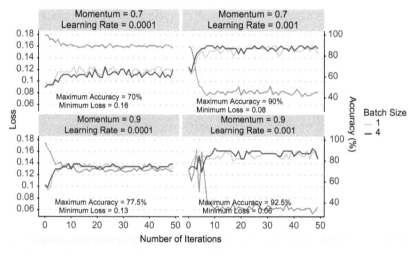

Figure 7.5 Loss and Accuracy for different learning rates, momentum factors, and batch sizes. *Results for models with a .001 and .0001 learning rate*

accuracy (60%). This is probably because the pretrained model is already close to finding the most accurate model and big "jumps" through the parameter space do not help.

Figure 7.5 also indicates that models with the intermediate learning rate of 0.001 perform better than those with faster and slower rates. It is also interesting to note that models with a higher momentum factors tend to do better. Finally, batch size also does not appear to have a consistent effect on model accuracy. Informed by these results, we test three intermediate learning rates when fine-tuning the seven other binary classifiers: 0.005, 0.001, and 0.0005. Because the initial results were indeterminate as to the best momentum factor and batch size, we will continue to vary these hyperparameters. As for the appropriate number of epochs, most of the models reached convergence after about 10 epochs. More than 50 would seem to be a waste of computing power in this case.

7.6 Results

We are now ready to fine-tune ResNet-18 to build each of the seven binary classifiers. For each classifier, we replace the last fully connected $1 \times 1 \times 1000$ layer with a layer fitting our needs (a $1 \times 1 \times 2$ layer for the binary classifiers) and we retrain the CNN for 50 epochs using a 0.1 gamma and a step size of 7. For each of the seven classifiers we experiment with three intermediate learning rates (0.0005, 0.001, and 0.005), two momentum factors (0.9 and 0.7), and two batch sizes (1 and 4 images).

We judge performance on the validation set using four common measures in machine learning: recall, precision, F1-score, and accuracy. As a reminder, *precision* is the proportion of predicted positive cases that are correct (when compared to a set of gold standard labels); *recall* is the proportion of true positive cases that are correctly predicted to be positive cases; the *F1-score* provides a performance summary accounting for both precision and recall $(2 \times \dfrac{precision \times recall}{precision + recall})$; and *accuracy* is the overall proportion of predicted positive and negative cases that are correctly predicted. As a reminder, these are all balanced sets with the same number of true positives and negatives, so if the CNNs were predicting at random they would be getting it right 50% of the time. This 50% baseline is the one we need to keep in mind when judging the results.

The best results from our experiments for each classifier task are reported in Table 7.2. The first thing to note is that accuracy varies substantially across the different tasks, from 1.00 for the protest classifier to 0.64 for the enthusiasm one. A second point is that the best performing learning rate, batch size, and momentum factor varies across the tasks.[38] For example, the protest classifier achieved the best accuracy with a momentum factor of 0.9, while a momentum factor of 0.7 was best for the disgust classifier.

7.6.1 Object Recognition Results

Fine-tuning Resnet-18 to predict protest images produced excellent results (accuracy, precision, and recall of 100%) with just 100 true positive and 100

---

[38] Readers replicating these efforts will obtain slightly different results because the image batches used at each iteration are randomized.

Table 7.2 Best Results for Fine-Tuning Experiments

Classifier	Accuracy	F1-Score	Precision	Recall	Learning Rate	Momentum Factor	Batch Size
Protest	1.00	1.00	1.00	1.00	0.0005	0.9	1
John Legend	0.92	0.92	0.95	0.90	0.0005	0.9	1
Anger	0.70	0.71	0.68	0.75	0.0050	0.9	4
Disgust	0.71	0.68	0.75	0.62	0.0005	0.7	4
Fear	0.70	0.67	0.75	0.60	0.0050	0.9	1
Enthusiasm	0.63	0.61	0.64	0.58	0.0005	0.7	4
Sadness	0.68	0.71	0.64	0.78	0.0005	0.9	1

true negative training examples. Of course, this is just one experiment and not necessarily representative of how well a fine-tuned CNN will perform in predicting all other new labels. The positive and negative cases in this example were relatively distinct. In other cases, for example distinguishing between images of parade crowds and protesting crowds, or distinguishing between a broad range of protest activities (e.g., a Greenpeace protester hanging from Mt. Rushmore versus a marching crowd), training an accurate classifier might prove more challenging.

7.6.2 Facial Recognition Results

The results for the John Legend classifier (92% accuracy, precision of 95%, and recall of 90%) are also very good, particularly given the small training sample (100 true positives and 100 true negatives). Overall accuracy is slightly lower than for protests (100%) and for Rekognition (99.4%). These differences in overall accuracy illustrate the benefits of having more images for train/testing. We assume that Rekognition is trained on a very large set of celebrity face images. In addition, the Rekognition algorithm uses face detection to segment each individual face in an image whereas our task did not entail any image segmentation. Why use fine-tuning for this task then, if Rekognition was more accurate? The simple answer is that Rekognition may not have a label or a substantial number of training examples for your person of interest. When this is the case, fine-tuning will be a better, and still highly accurate, option.

7.6.3 Visual Sentiment Results

Given that the baseline performance for a binary classifier with a balanced train-validation set is 50% (a coin toss), all our example classifiers on evoked emotion are only somewhat successful, with F1-scores ranging from 68% to 71%. This is clearly not as accurate as the object and facial recognition classifiers.

The emotions tasks are inherently more challenging than recognizing an object or face. Computer vision scholars have been able to build similarly accurate (60–70% accuracy) binary emotion classifiers using very large training corpora (Peng et al. 2015), but the images used for these classifiers have very simple compositions (see examples from the Emotion6 dataset available here).[39] Politically relevant images that people share online are often more complex. For example, our BLM dataset includes images of cartoons, images with several elements, and images combining visuals with text (see examples here[40] or readers can view the training data in the accompanying Code Ocean capsule).[41] This greater diversity of images means that larger training sets of politically relevant images and possibly more complex models (for example, models that incorporate object detection, facial detection, and text analysis) may be needed to make substantial progress in predicting the emotional impact of political images. Although challenging, the potential research benefits of such a trained model are substantial.

7.7 Using a Fine-Tuned Classifier to Label New Images

The final step in an application of fine-tuning is to use the trained and validated model to label additional images. This step is no different than applying any trained off-the-shelf algorithm to new data. Code available in the Github repo demonstrates how to load a trained model and apply it to a different set of images.[42]

7.8 Extended Application: Multilevel Classifier

What if a researcher wanted to predict whether an image belonged to one of many possible classes rather than a single class? With our fine-tuning

---

[39] https://norawebbwilliams.github.io/ce_images/emotion6_anger_example.jpg, last accessed April 26, 2020.

[40] https://norawebbwilliams.github.io/ce_images/blm_anger_example.jpg, last accessed April 26, 2020.

[41] https://doi.org/10.24433/CO.2462313.v1, last accessed April 26, 2020 (Webb Williams, Casas, and Wilkerson 2020).

[42] https://github.com/norawebbwilliams/images_as_data/blob/master/code/04-apply-finetuned-cnn-to-new-images.py, last accessed April 26, 2020 (Webb Williams and Casas 2020).

framework, the only difference to train a multiclass classifier is in the adjustment to the final layer of the pretrained Resnet-18. Instead of adjusting the last layer of the algorithm from 1000 categories to 2, a researcher would adjust the algorithm into the number of classes appropriate for their case. We test a multiclass classifier using a toy corpus of images of world leaders from six countries (the USA, Venezuela, South Africa, Japan, Kazakhstan, and Spain). Thus, in this case we adjust the last layer of Resnet-18 to six classes.

We collected 50 images of each leader from online sources and then cropped them to include only the face (see examples here[43] or readers can view the training data in the accompanying Code Ocean capsule).[44] The example code for a multilevel classifier is available in the accompanying Github repo, in either the code[45] or the notebook directory[46] or on Code Ocean.[47] As with the binary classifiers, it is worth experimenting with different hyperparameter combinations to improve accuracy.

7.8.1 Directory Structure for Multilevel Classifier

For the binary models, each subdirectory in the "data" directory contained a set of true positive and true negative images for the binary feature of interest. For a multilevel classifier, instead of having subdirectories of images that do and do not include a protest, each subdirectory includes images of only one of the six leaders (as illustrated below). Once again, we use 80% of the images for training and 20% for testing.

- "train": contains the images used for training, with subdirectories for:
  - "USA": 40 images of Barack Obama
  - "VEN": 40 images of Nicolas Maduro
  - "ZAF": 40 images of Jacob Zuma
  - "JPN": 40 images of Shinzo Abe
  - "KAZ": 40 images of Nursultan Nazarbayev
  - "ESP": 40 images of Mariano Rajoy
- "val": contains images used for testing, with subdirectories for:

---

[43] https://norawebbwilliams.github.io/ce_images/leaders-examples.jpg, last accessed April 26, 2020.

[44] https://doi.org/10.24433/CO.2462313.v1, last accessed April 26, 2020 (Webb Williams, Casas, and Wilkerson 2020).

[45] https://github.com/norawebbwilliams/images_as_data/blob/master/code/02-fine-tune-multiclass-model.py, last accessed April 26, 2020 (Webb Williams and Casas 2020).

[46] https://github.com/norawebbwilliams/images_as_data/blob/master/notebooks/02-fine-tune-multiclass-model.ipynb, last accessed April 26, 2020 (Webb Williams and Casas 2020).

[47] https://doi.org/10.24433/CO.2462313.v1, last accessed April 26, 2020 (Webb Williams, Casas, and Wilkerson 2020).

- "USA": 10 images of Barack Obama
- "VEN": 10 images of Nicolas Maduro
- "ZAF": 10 images of Jacob Zuma
- "JPN": 10 images of Shinzo Abe
- "KAZ": 10 images of Nursultan Nazarbayev
- "ESP": 10 images of Mariano Rajoy

7.8.2 Multilevel Classifier Results

After just 50 epochs, the model achieved perfect accuracy, precision, and recall for all six classes. Admittedly, we simplified the task by cropping the images so that they focused exclusively on the leaders' heads and faces. Nevertheless, we still find this success rate impressive. With minimal training (a small number of examples and epochs), the algorithm successfully distinguished among six different people who were not included as part of the original ResNet-18 training data.

8 Legal and Ethical Concerns in Using Images as Data

In this section we encourage readers to consider the legal and ethical implications of using images in research. Many image analysis projects raise competing considerations of research reproducibility, transparency, privacy, risks of causing harm, and copyright protections. Researchers need to be aware of potential legal and ethical issues related to the gathering, storing, and processing of images and should consult with their organization's legal team, if available, to ensure compliance with current law and best practices. Institutional Review Boards (IRBs) are an important first and necessary step, but their policies may lag behind ethical best practices for social media research (Moreno et al. 2013). For this reason we also recommend reading through the resources curated by the Association for Computing Machinery Conference on Fairness, Accountability, and Transparency (ACM FAccT).[48]

8.1 Fair Use of Copyright Protected Images

Social media terms of service generally acknowledge that the person or organization that posts content (text, image, video, etc.) retains ownership of that content. This helps networks avoid liability for what is posted on their sites. Courts have also affirmed this copyright protection in cases involving other parties' commercial use of such images (Ax 2013). However, in the United States (Title 17, Section 107 of the US Code), *fair use* of protected content

---

[48] https://facctconference.org/links.html, last accessed April 26, 2020 (*ACM FAccT - Links* 2020).

for purposes such as "criticism, comment, news reporting, teaching (including multiple copies for classroom use), scholarship, or research" is protected. Researchers (and editors) should nevertheless proceed with caution because copyright violation claims are considered on a case-by-case basis and because policies may vary across domains and legal contexts.

For example, the European Union is currently considering changes to its "Directive on Copyright in the Digital Single Market." Proposed changes to Articles 11 and 13, for example, would strengthen copyright protections for those who create material later shared online. These changes seem to be primarily directed at commercial uses, but the policies had not been finalized at the time of this writing. Certainly the safest course of action, one consistent with opinions expressed in public surveys, is for researchers to either obtain permission or alter images before including them in published works. One advantage of using social media is that it can be relatively easy to contact account holders for permission.

In addition, uses that are legal are not always ethical. We highlight three additional concerns related to image research that fall primarily in the realm of ethics (at least for now): privacy, harm, and social algorithmic bias.

8.2 Privacy

Polls indicate that the public is generally supportive of academic research but that it is also concerned about protecting privacy when it comes to social media data. Surveying social media users, Williams, Burnap, and Sloan (2017) found that "84% of respondents were not at all or only slightly concerned" (p. 1156) about the use of their information in university research settings. However, "[j]ust under 80 per cent of respondents agreed that they would expect to be asked for their consent before their Twitter posts were published in academic outputs. Over 90 per cent of respondents agreed that they would want to remain anonymous in publications stemming from Twitter research based in university settings" (Williams, Burnap, and Sloan 2017, p. 1156).

Recent scandals involving academic researchers have drawn renewed attention to such privacy concerns (see the scandals referenced by M. Rosenberg, Confessore, and Cadwalladr 2018 and Suppe 2018). In partial response, some online social networks have imposed restrictions on data collection. Instagram, for example, the popular social network owned by Facebook where users post images almost exclusively, now has a strict set of policies for those who use their API ("platform policy," "terms of service," or "terms of use").[49] Their

---

[49] www.instagram.com/developer/, last accessed April 26, 2020.

policy states, for example, that "you cannot use the API Platform to crawl or store users' media without their express consent."

As with copyright protections, laws on data privacy will vary by country and legal context. For example, any researcher collecting or using data from Europe also needs to be aware of recent new requirements from the European Union's General Data Protection Regulation (GDPR).[50] The GDPR still allows for research-oriented use of personal data, but scholars should seek legal advice or read up on background materials to make sure their project is properly carried out.[51]

Once images have been collected, researchers also need to be attentive to how they are stored and shared. This is one place where scientific concerns about research reproducibility can conflict with ethical concerns about privacy. What are the privacy implications of publicly sharing images used in research, especially when those images are categorized by topic or event?

For example, Twitter images are already in the public sphere and available for anyone to collect. Does aggregating them for an academic research project increase the potential for harm or violate privacy norms? This could be the case if, for example, the results from a project using CNNs to predict sexual orientation were shared publicly, regardless of whether the images contained additional identifying information or not. For such a project, we believe that prior consent is required before sharing the images because someone might be dangerously "outed."

On the other hand, creating and sharing a collection of protest images drawn from Twitter for research purposes seems less likely to increase harm because people who participate in public protests can reasonably expect to be photographed. Of course, such a project would arguably become unethical (absent user consent) if the objective was to develop an algorithm making it easier to identify individual protest participants. The development and sharing of such technologies could ultimately facilitate government surveillance and repression (Introna and Wood 2004). Owen (2018) provides a helpful popular press account of the ethics of automatic facial recognition.

Another privacy issue arises with the use of off-the-shelf tools like Amazon's Rekognition. When they use these tools to label images, researchers may effectively transfer protected content to a commercial service. It is our understanding that images uploaded to such services are added to the service's

---

[50] https://ec.europa.eu/commission/priorities/justice-and-fundamental-rights/data-protection/2018-reform-eu-data-protection-rules_en, last accessed April 26, 2020 (European Commission 2020).

[51] See, for example, Lancaster University (2020) and University of Oxford (2020).

repository, along with the assigned labels. This is probably also the case for other commercial services that enable researchers to train CNNs for specific image tasks (along the lines of the fine-tuning discussed in this Element), such as Google's AutoML Vision.[52] We cannot recommend these services to researchers concerned about protecting privacy if they do not offer the option of permanently deleting data and results. Open-source taggers that researchers download and run locally, such as face_recognition (Geitgey 2020), do not present the same privacy concerns.

8.3 Causing Harm

Researchers also need to be concerned about other harms associated with image sharing besides violations of individual privacy. Here we discuss two related areas of concern: harm caused by sharing images and harm caused to those who might be exposed to disturbing images during the research process.

Most social media services attempt to filter content that is especially offensive, including sexually explicit images and images containing graphic violence or death. In some cases, these images are posted with the implicit intent of causing harm (for example, what is colloquially referred to as "revenge porn"). Researchers need to seriously consider whether their research projects might inadvertently increase harm by preserving harmful images or increasing the likelihood of exposure to such explicit images.

In addition to general sharing issues, the harm may be more direct when, for example, a researcher employs undergraduate research assistants or a crowdsourcing service. Prescreening images before assigning them, establishing a minimum hiring age, and briefing research assistants about what they may encounter can all help. Mechanical Turk, for example, requires specific language[53] if a task may include explicit content: "(WARNING: This HIT may contain adult content. Worker discretion is advised.)"

Similar warnings may be appropriate when images are shared for the purposes of replication/reproducibility. Alternatively, a researcher may choose to exclude certain images from a project, or filter the images that are used as illustrations of the methodology. For example, our original binary emotions classifiers image dataset included some explicit images (14 images containing either explicit sexual nudity or graphic violence). These images were valuable for training and testing the classifiers (specifically their ability to detect "disgust" or "fear"); however, we exclude them from the data that accompany the replication files in Github and Code Ocean.

---

[52] https://cloud.google.com/vision/, last accessed April 26, 2020.
[53] www.mturk.com/acceptable-use-policy, last accessed April 26, 2020.

One approach to balancing reproducibility and privacy concerns is to provide only the information needed to recreate the dataset used in the study. In the case of Twitter, each tweet has a unique id. Instead of sharing the collected tweets and their associated media (images, video, etc.) from a project, the researcher can share the list of collected tweet ids (for an example see Clarke and Kocak [2018]). This approach offers additional privacy protection to Twitter users. If they decide to delete their tweets, their posts will not continue to be shared in a researcher's dataset. On the other hand, this approach raises potential issues of reproducibility. If the deleted tweets drove the results of the initial study, the findings might not replicate. Similarly, an unethical researcher could claim that a set of results would hold with a complete replication, or could even create and subsequently delete tweets to support a particular result.

8.4 Social Algorithmic Bias

Finally, an important research agenda is demonstrating that machine learning algorithms (including computer vision algorithms) are only as good as their training data and classification schemes. If training data reflect conscious or unconscious biases, the trained systems will learn that bias. Most concerning is a potential for these algorithms to not only reproduce societal and cognitive biases but to exacerbate them. For example, Zhao et al. (2017) finds that AI trained on a set of Internet images was likely to assign women to the activity of "cooking" at much higher rates than occurred in the original data set (cooking was more about 33% more likely to include women than men in the train data; this rate rose to 68% with the trained model). In another example, the Gender Shades[54] project (Buolamwini and Gebru 2018) shows that AI systems are much worse at correctly identifying gender with nonwhite faces.

Researchers need to understand why these biases can occur and think carefully about the potential social biases of their own research designs. Google's answer to the controversy of its image tagger returning the label "gorilla" when applied to black faces was to suppress the tag (Simonite 2018). While this solution might blunt some criticism, it does not solve the problem. To prevent social bias, researchers should be aware of the issues and continue to push their own work to be ethical and free from biases. For further high-level reading on the topic, we suggest Broussard (2018), Kearns and Roth (2019), and O'Neil (2017).

---

[54] http://gendershades.org/, last accessed April 26, 2020 (*Gender Shades* 2020).

9 Conclusion

Images are an important part of everyday political and social life and they deserve more attention from social scientists. Prior research demonstrates that images can be a powerful form of communication. Compared to text, visuals are more likely to capture people's attention, trigger strong emotional reactions, and improve information recall. The computer vision methods discussed in this Element can be used to study images at scale, making it possible to explore the impact of images in real-world contexts (as opposed to more limited and controlled experimental settings).

There have been tremendous advances in computer vision research over the last decade and resources such as Amazon's Rekognition service and the PyTorch deep-learning framework mean that non–computer scientists can now take advantage of these developments. Many commercial and open-source off-the-shelf autotaggers have already been trained to predict a very large number of popular image labels. These off-the-shelf options may be perfectly suitable for many image-related research projects, depending on the task. A plus is that they do not require manually labeled examples except for validation, but potential downsides include omitted labels, questionable classification reproducibility, and copyright and privacy violations.

Fine-tuning can be a better option when the labels and underlying data of an autotagger do not match the goals of a research project. As with any machine learning task, the success of a fine-tuning effort will depend on the complexity of the task, the representativeness of the training data, and modeling decisions the researcher must make along the way. Pretrained CNNs lower the bar in terms of the investment required to obtain labeled images in order to test theoretical questions of interest, greatly expanding research opportunities.

Because the goal of image classification is typically prediction rather than explanation, researchers are free to experiment with a large number of available hyperparameters and open-source CNNs. Even if an adjustment only leads to a modest improvement, it is still an improvement, and many modest improvements can make a real difference in accuracy. We have demonstrated some implications of hyperparameter decisions, but this is an area where constant experimentation via grid search is warranted.

Some labeling tasks, such as predicting emotional responses, are more difficult than others because they are subjective or because the relevant attributes (the features that produce the emotional response) are less distinguishable using pixel-level information alone. Building a model that can capture the general features of diverse images that make people angry is substantially more difficult than recognizing the fairly standard facial features of a given celebrity. In the examples presented in this Element, our fine-tuning produced fairly unsuccessful CNNs for this visual sentiment analysis task. With more training data and more involved pipelines, it is possible that these complicated classes will become easy to predict. However, the challenges of visual sentiment analysis also reveal the potential limits of these techniques. Automated image analysis for highly subjective labels may be beyond what is possible with current methods.

Our main goal in this introduction to computer vision methods is to inspire social scientists to devote more attention to the role of large quantities of digitized visuals in political and social life. An important aspect to conducting this research is ethical concerns, which can arise at every stage of an images-as-data project. As a research community, we should always be aware of the potential for harm that our studies might bring, from violating privacy norms to reinforcing social biases.

10 Data Availability Statement

The data and the code to run the examples given in this Element are available on Github and Code Ocean.

Github: https://github.com/norawebbwilliams/images_as_data

Code Ocean: https://doi.org/10.24433/CO.2462313.v1

References

A Neural Network Playground (2020). https://playground.tensorflow.org/#acti
vation=tanh&batchSize=10&dataset=circle&regDataset=reg-plane&lear
ningRate=0.03&regularizationRate=0&noise=0&networkShape=4,2&se
ed=0.81811&showTestData=false&discretize=false&percTrainData=50
&x=true&y=true&xTimesY=fal (last accessed April 26, 2020).

ACM FAccT – Links (2020). https://facctconference.org/links.html (last accessed April 26, 2020).

Anastasopoulos, L. J. ct al. (2016). "Photographic Home Styles in Congress:
A Computer Vision Approach," Approach," 1–52. http://arxiv.org/abs/
1611.09942.

Ax, J. (2013). *Photographer Wins $1.2 million from Companies That Took
Pictures off Twitter* www.reuters.com/article/us-media-copyright-twitter/
photographer-wins-1-2-million-from-companies-that-took-pictures-off-
twitter-idUSBRE9AL16F20131122.

Bennett, W. L., and A. Segerberg (2013). *The Logic of Connective Action: Digital Media and the Personalization of Contentious Politics*. New York:
Cambridge University Press.

Benoit, K., et al. (2016). "Crowd-sourced Text Analysis: Reproducible and
Agile Production of Political Data." *American Political Science Review*
110(2), 278–295.

Bimber, B., A. J. Flanagin, and C. Stohl (2005). "Reconceptualizing Collective Action in the Contemporary Media Environment." *Communication Theory* 15(4), 365–388. http://doi.wiley.com/10.1111/j.1468-2885
.2005.tb00340.x.

Brantner, C., K. Lobinger, and W. Irmgard (2011). "Effects of Visual Framing
on Emotional Responses and Evaluations of News Stories about the Gaza
Conflict 2009." *Journalism & Mass Communication Quarterly* 88(3),
523–540.

Britz, D. (2015). *Understanding Convolutional Neural Networks for NLP –
WildML*. www.wildml.com/2015/11/understanding-convolutional-neural
-networks-for-nlp/ (last accessed April 26, 2020).

Broussard, M. (2018). *Artificial Unintelligence: How Computers Misunder-
stand the World*. Cambridge, MA: The Massachusetts Institute of Technology Press.

Budhiraja, A. (2016). *Dropout in (Deep) Machine Learning – Amar Budhiraja
– Medium*. URL: https://medium.com/@amarbudhiraja/https-medium

-com-amarbudhiraja-learning-less-to-learn-better-dropout-in-deep-mach ine-learning-74334da4bfc5 (last accessed April 26, 2020).

Buduma, N., and N. Locascio (2017). *Fundamentals of Deep Learning: Designing Next-generation Machine Intelligence Algorithms*. Sebastopol, CA: O'Reilly Media.

Buolamwini, J., and T. Gebru (2018). "Gender Shades: Intersectional Accuracy Disparities in Commercial Gender Classification." In: *Proceedings of Machine Learning Research*. Vol. 81, pp. 1–15.

Burns, N., et al. (2011). "Sentiment Analysis of Customer Reviews: Balanced versus Unbalanced Datasets." In: *Knowledge-Based and Intelligent Information and Engineering Systems* Ed. by A. König et al. Berlin, Heidelberg: Springer Berlin Heidelberg, pp. 161–170.

Callen, M., and J. D. Long (2015). "Institutional Corruption and Election Fraud: Evidence from a Field Experiment in Afghanistan." *American Economic Review* 105(1), 354–381.

Cantú, F. (2019). "The Fingerprints of Fraud: Evidence from Mexico's 1988 Presidential Election." *American Political Science Review*. Vol. 113, Issue 3, pp. 710–726.

Casas, A., and N. Webb Williams (2018). "Images that Matter: Online Protests and the Mobilizing Role of Pictures." *Political Research Quarterly*, Vol. 72, Issue 2, 360–375.

Casas, A., et al. (2019). "Visual Clustering: A Technique for Drastically Reducing Image Annotation Tasks." Presented at Annual Meeting of the International Communication Association, Washington, D.C.

Castells, M. (2012). *Networks of Outrage and Hope: Social Movements in the Internet Age*. Cambridge, UK; Malden, MA: Polity Press.

Cillizza, C. (2018). *Melania Trump's 'I Really Don't Care. Do U?' Jacket Was No Mistake- - CNNPolitics*. www.cnn.com/2018/06/21/politics/melania-trump-jacket-border-visit/index.html (last accessed April 26, 2020).

Clarke, K., and K. Kocak (2018). *Replication Data for: Launching Revolution: Social Media and the Egyptian Uprising's First Movers*. https://doi .org/10.7910/DVN/S17DDJ.

COCO – Common Objects in Context (2020). http://cocodataset.org/#home (last accessed April 26, 2020).

Corrigall-Brown, C., and R. Wilkes (2012). "Picturing Protest: The Visual Framing of Collective Action by First Nations in Canada." *American Behavioral Scientist* 56(2), 223–243.

CS231n Convolutional Neural Networks for Visual Recognition (2020). https:// cs231n.github.io/ (last accessed April 25, 2020).

Dahmen, N. S. (2012). "Photographic Framing in the Stem Cell Debate." *American Behavioral Scientist* 56(2), 189–203.

Dietrich, B. J. (2019). "Using Motion Detection to Measure Social Polarization in the U.S. House of Representatives."

Domhan, T., J. Springenberg, and F. Hutter (2015). "Speeding Up Automatic Hyperparameter Optimization of Deep Neural Networks by Extrapolation of Learning Curves". IJCAI'15: Proceedings of the 24th International Conference on Artificial Intelligence, pp. 3460–3468

European Commission (2020). *EU Data Protection Rules.* https://ec.europa.eu/info/priorities/justice-and-fundamental-rights/data-protection/2018-refo rm-eu-data-protection-rules/eu-data-protection-rules_en (last accessed April 26, 2020).

Geitgey, A. (2020). *ageitgey/face_recognition: The World's Simplest Facial Recognition API for Python and the Command Line.* https://github .com/ageitgey/face_recognition (last accessed April 26, 2020).

Gelman, A., and J. Hill (2007). *Data Analysis Using Regression and Multilevel/Hierarchical Models.* New York, NY: Cambridge University Press.

Gender Shades (2020). http://gendershades.org/ (last accessed April 26, 2020).

Girshick, R. B. (2015). "Fast {R-CNN}." *CoRR* abs/1504.0. http://arxiv.org/abs/1504.08083.

Girshick, R. B., et al. (2013). "Rich Feature Hierarchies for Accurate Object Detection and Semantic Segmentation." *CoRR* abs/1311.2. http://arxiv.org/abs/1311.2524.

Gitlin, T. (1980). *The Whole World Is Watching: Mass Media in the Making and Unmaking of the New Left.* Berkeley: University of California Press.

Goh, G. (2017). "Why Momentum Really Works." *Distill.* http://distill .pub/2017/momentum.

Golle, P. (2008). "Machine Learning Attacks against the Asirra CAPTCHA." In: *CCS '08 Proceedings of the 15th ACM Conference on Computer and Communications Security*, pp. 535–542.

Grabe, M. E., and E. P. Bucy (2009). *Image Bite Politics: News and the Visual Framing of Elections.* Oxford; New York: Oxford University Press.

Guo, Y., et al. (2016). "MS-Celeb-1M: A Dataset and Benchmark for Large-Scale Face Recognition." In: *European Conference on Computer Vision (ECCV).* www.hdwallpapers.in/anne.

Hamner, B. (2019). *2016 US Election | Kaggle.* www.kaggle.com/benham ner/2016-us-election (last accessed April 26, 2020).

He, K., G. Gkioxari, et al. (2017). "Mask {R-CNN}." *CoRR* abs/1703.0. http://arxiv.org/abs/1703.06870.

He, K., X. Zhang, et al. (2015). "Deep Residual Learning for Image Recognition." In: *arXiv:1512.03385*.

Henderson, J. V., A. Storeygard, and D. N. Weil (2012). "Measuring Economic Growth from Outer Space Author." *American Economic Review* 102(2), 994–1028.

Horiuchi, Y., T. Komatsu, and F. Nakaya (2012). "Should Candidates Smile to Win Elections? An Application of Automated Face Recognition Technology." *Political Psychology* 33(6), 925–933.

Howard, P. N., and M. M. Hussain (2013). *Democracy's Fourth Wave?: Digital Media and the Arab Spring*. New York, NY: Oxford University Press.

Hwang, J., K. Imai, and A. Tarr (2019). "Automated Coding of Political Campaign Advertisement Videos: An Empirical Validation Study." Kosuke Imai's Homepage. https://imai.fas.harvard.edu/research/files/campvideo.pdf.

ImageNet (2020). http://image-net.org/ (last accessed April 26, 2020).

Internet Live Stats – Internet Usage & Social Media Statistics (2020). www.internetlivestats.com/ (last accessed April 26, 2020).

Introna, L. D., and D. Wood (2004). "Picturing Algorithmic Surveillance: The Politics of Facial Recognition Systems." *Surveillance and Society* 2(2–3), 177–198.

Iyer, A., and J. Oldmeadow (2006). "Picture This: Emotional and Political Responses to Photographs of the Kenneth Bigley Kidnapping." *European Journal of Social Psychology* 36(5), 635–647.

Jean, N., et al. (2016). "Combining Satellite Imagery and Machine Learning to Predict Poverty." *Science* 353(6301), 790–794. www.ncbi.nlm.nih.gov/pubmed/27540167.

Joo, J., E. P. Bucy, and C. Seidel (2019). "Automated Coding of Televised Leader Displays: Detecting Nonverbal Political Behavior with Computer Vision and Deep Learning." *International Journal of Communication*. Vol. 19, pp. 4044–4066.

Joo, J., W. Li, et al. (2014). "Visual Persuasion: Inferring Communicative Intents of Images." In: *Proceedings of the IEEE Conference on Computer Vision and Pattern Recognition*. IEEE, pp. 216–223.

Joo, J., F. F. Steen, and S.-C. Zhu (2015). "Automated Facial Trait Judgment and Election Outcome Prediction: Social Dimensions of Face." In: *Proceedings of the IEEE International Conference on Computer Vision*. IEEE, pp. 3712–3720.

Kaufman, A., G. King, and M. Komisarchik (2019). "How to Measure Legislative District Compactness If You Only Know It When You See it."

Kearns, M., and A. Roth (2019). *The Ethical Algorithm: The Science of Socially Aware Algorithm Design* Oxford: Oxford University Press.

Kharroub, T., and O. Bas (2015). "Social Media and Protests: An Examination of Twitter Images of the 2011 Egyptian Revolution." *New Media & Society* 18(9): 1973–1992. http://nms.sagepub.com/cgi/doi/10.1177/1461444815571914.

Krizhevsky, A., I. Sutskever, and G. E. Hinton (2012). "ImageNet Classification with Deep Convolutional Neural Networks." In: *Advances in Neural Information Processing Systems*, pp. 1106–1114.

Kulkarni, G., et al. (2013). "BabyTalk: Understanding and Generating Simple Image Descriptions." *IEEE Transactions on Pattern Analysis and Machine Intelligence* 35(12), 2891–2903.

Lam, O., et al. (2019). *Men Appear Twice as Often as Women in News Photos on Facebook.* Tech. rep. Pew Research Center. www.journalism.org/2019/05/23/men-appear-twice-as-often-as-women-in-news-photos-on-facebook/.

Lancaster University (2020). *GDPR: What Researchers Need to Know | Lancaster University.* www.lancaster.ac.uk/research/research-services/research-integrity-ethics–governance/data-protection/gdpr-what-researchers-need-to-know/ (last accessed April 26, 2020).

LeCun, Y., Y. Bengio, and G. Hinton (2015). "Deep Learning." *Nature* 521(7553), 436–444.

Li, H., et al. (2015). "A Convolutional Neural Network Cascade for Face Detection." In: *2015 IEEE Conference on Computer Vision and Pattern Recognition.*

Lin, T. Y., et al. (2014). "Microsoft COCO: Common Objects in Context." In: *Lecture Notes in Computer Science (including subseries Lecture Notes in Artificial Intelligence and Lecture Notes in Bioinformatics).* Vol. 8693 LNCS. PART 5. Springer Verlag, pp. 740–755.

Marcus, G. E., W. R. Neuman, and M. MacKuen (2000). *Affective Intelligence and Political Judgement.* Chicago and London: University of Chicago Press.

Mebane, W. R. J., et al. (2017). "Using Twitter to Observe Election Incidents in the United States." (Paper presented at the 2016 Annual Meeting of the Midwest Political Science Association, Chicago, April 6–9, 2017)

Messaris, P., and L. Abraham (2001). "The Role of Images in Framing News Stories." In: *Framing Public Life: Perspectives on Media and Our Understanding of the Social World.* Ed. by Reese, Stephen D., Gandy, Oscar H., and A. E. Grant. Mahwah, NJ: Lawrence Erlbaum Associates Publishers, pp. 215–226.

Metz, C. (2019). *Facial Recognition Tech Is Growing Stronger, Thanks to Your Face*. www.nytimes.com/2019/07/13/technology/databases-faces-facial-recognition-technology.html?searchResultPosition=7.

Moreno, M. A., et al. (2013). "Ethics of Social Media Research: Common Concerns and Practical Considerations". *Cyberpsychology, Behavior, and Social Networking* 16(9), 708–713. URL: http://online.liebertpub .com/doi/abs/10.1089/cyber.2012.0334.

Mountassir, A., Benbrahim Hourda, and I. Berrada (2012). "An Empirical Study to Address the Problem of Unbalanced Data Sets in Sentiment Classification." In: *2012 IEEE International Conference on Systems, Man, and Cybernetics (SMC)*, pp. 3298–3303.

MS-Celeb-1M: Challenge of Recognizing One Million Celebrities in the Real World-Microsoft Research (2020). www.microsoft.com/en-us/ research/project/ms-celeb-1m-challenge-recognizing-one-million-celeb rities-real-world/ (last accessed April 26, 2020).

Nanne, A., et al. (2019). "The Use of Computer Vision to Analyze Visual Brand-Related User Generated Content: A Comparison of YOLOV2, Google Cloud Vision, and Clarifai." *Journal of Interactive Marketing* 50, 156–167.

Nelson, D. L., V. S. Reed, and J. R. Walling (1976). "Pictorial Superiority Effect." *Journal of Experimental Psychology: Human Learning and Memory* 2(5), 523–528.

O'Neil, C. (2017). *Weapons of Math Destruction: How Big Data Increases Inequality and Threatens Democracy* New York: Broadway Books.

Owen, D. (2018). "Should We Be Worried About Computerized Facial Recognition?" *The New Yorker.* www.newyorker.com/magazine/2018/12/ 17/should-we-be-worried-about-computerized-facial-recognition.

Paivio, A., T. B. Rogers, and P. C. Smythe (1968). "Why Are Pictures Easier to Recall Than Words?" *Psychonomic Science* 11(4), 137–138.

Peng, K.-c., et al. (2015). "A Mixed Bag of Emotions: Model, Predict, and Transfer Emotion Distributions." In: *2015 IEEE Conference on Computer Vision and Pattern Recognition (CVPR)* pp. 1–9.

Peng, Y. (2018). "Same Candidates, Different Faces: Uncovering Media Bias in Visual Portrayals of Presidential Candidates with Computer Vision." *Journal of Communication* 68(5), 920–941.

(2020). *COMPUTER VISION – YILANG PENG*. https://yilangpeng.com/ computer-vision/ (last accessed April 26, 2020).

Philipp, H., C. Müller-Crepon, and L.-E. Cederman (n.d.). "Roads to Rule, Roads to Rebel: Relational State Capacity and Conflict in Africa."

Powell, T., et al. (2015). "A Clearer Picture: The Contribution of Visuals and Text to Framing Effects." *Journal of Communication* 65(6), 997–1017.

Project Jupyter | Home (2020). https://jupyter.org/ (last accessed April 26, 2020).

Raiford, L. (2007). "World Together: SNCC and Photography of the Civil Rights Movement." *American Quarterly* 59(4), 1129–1157.

Redmon, J., S. Divvala, et al. (2016). "You Only Look Once: Unified, Real-Time Object Detection." In: *2016 IEEE Conference on Computer Vision and Pattern Recognition (CVPR)*, pp. 779–788.

Redmon, J., and A. Farhadi (2018). "YOLOv3: An Incremental Improvement." https://arxiv.org/abs/1804.02767.

Ren, S., et al. (2015). "Faster {R-CNN:} Towards Real-Time Object Detection with Region Proposal Networks." *CoRR* abs/1506.0. http://arxiv.org/abs/1506.01497.

Ribeiro, M. T., S. Singh, and C. Guestrin (2016). " 'Why Should I Trust You?': Explaining the Predictions of Any Classifier." In: *Proceedings of the 22Nd ACM SIGKDD International Conference on Knowledge Discovery and Data Mining*. KDD '16. New York, N: ACM, pp. 1135–1144. http://doi.acm.org/10.1145/2939672.2939778.

Rosenberg, M., N. Confessore, and C. Cadwalladr (2018). "How Trump Consultants Exploited the Facebook Data of Millions." *The New York Times*. www.nytimes.com/2018/03/17/us/politics/cambridge-analytica-trump-campaign.html.

Rosenberg, S. W., et al. (1986). "The Image and the Vote: The Effect of Candidate Presentation on Voter Preference." *American Journal of Political Science* 30(1), 108–127.

Ruder, S. (2016). "An Overview of Gradient Descent Optimization Algorithms." *CoRR* abs/1609.0. http://arxiv.org/abs/1609.04747.

Russakovsky, O., et al. (2015). "ImageNet Large Scale Visual Recognition Challenge." *International Journal of Computer Vision (IJCV)* 115(3), 211–252.

Saldaña, J. (2009). *The Coding Manual for Qualitative Researchers*. Thousand Oaks, CA: Sage Publications Ltd.

Schmidhuber, J. (2015). "Deep Learning in Neural Networks: An Overview". Neural Networks 61, 85–117.

Simonite, T. (2017). *Machines Learn a Biased View of Women*. www.wired.com/story/machines-taught-by-photos-learn-a-sexist-view-of-women/ (last accessed April 26, 2020).

(2018). *When It Comes to Gorillas, Google Photos Remains Blind* www.wir ed.com/story/when-it-comes-to-gorillas-google-photos-remains-blind/ (last accessed April 26, 2020).

Smith, L. N. (2018). "A Disciplined Approach to Neural Network Hyper-parameters: Part 1 – Learning Rate, Batch Size, Momentum, and Weight Decay." http://arxiv.org/abs/1803.09820.

Smith, R. (2007). "An Overview of the Tesseract OCR Engine." In: *Proceedings of the International Conference on Document Analysis and Recognition, ICDAR.* Vol. 2, pp. 629–633.

Sobolev, A., et al. (n.d.). "News and Geolocated Social Media Accurately Measure Protest Size." *Cartography and Geographic Information Science* 41(3).

Srivastava, N., et al. (2014). "Dropout: A Simple Way to Prevent Neural Networks from Overfitting." *J. Mach. Learn. Res.* 15(1), 1929–1958. http://dl .acm.org/citation.cfm?id=2627435.2670313.

Steinert-Threlkeld, Z. C. (2018). *Twitter as Data.* Elements in Quantitative and Computational Methods for the Social Sciences. Cambridge: Cambridge University Press.

Steinert-Threlkeld, Z. C., and J. Joo (n.d.). "Event Data from Images."

Suppe, R. (2018). "Orlando Police Decide to Keep Testing Controversial Amazon Facial Recognition Program." *USA Today.* www.usatoday.com/story/ tech/2018/07/09/orlando-police-decide-keep-testing-amazon-facial-reco gnition-program/768507002/.

Tai, L., and M. Liu (2016). "Mobile Robots Exploration through CNN-Based Reinforcement Learning." *Robotics and Biomimetics* 3(1), 24. https://doi.org/10.1186/s40638-016-0055-x.

Tanksale, N. (2018). *Finding Good Learning Rate and The One Cycle Policy.* https://towardsdatascience.com/finding-good-learning-rate-and-the-one-cycle-policy-7159fe1db5d6 (last accessed April 26, 2020).

Taylor, L., and G. Nitschke (2017). "Improving Deep Learning using Generic Data Augmentation." *CoRR* abs/1708.0. http://arxiv.org/abs/1708.06020.

Tesseract documentation | Tesseract OCR (2020). https://tesseract-ocr.github .io/ (last accessed April 26, 2020).

Todorov, A., et al. (2005). "Inferences of Competence from Faces Predict Election Outcomes." *Science* 308(5728), 1623–1626.

torchvision.models — PyTorch Master Documentation (2020). https://pytorch .org/docs/stable/torchvision/models.html (last accessed April 26, 2020).

Torres, M. (2019). "Give Me the Full Picture: Using Computer Vision to Understand Visual Frames and Political Communication."

University of Oxford (2020). *Responsibilities under GDPR | Research Support.* https://researchsupport.admin.ox.ac.uk/policy/data/responsibilities (last accessed April 26, 2020).

Webb Williams, N., and A. Casas (2020). "norawebbwilliams/images_as_data: First Release." *Github.*

Webb Williams, N., A. Casas, and J. Wilkerson (2020). *Images as Data for Social Science Research.* https://codeocean.com/capsule/8598879/tree/v1.

Wickham, H. (2017). *tidyverse: Easily Install and Load the "Tidyverse."* https://cran.r-project.org/package=tidyverse.

Williams, M. L., P. Burnap, and L. Sloan (2017). "Towards an Ethical Framework for Publishing Twitter Data in Social Research: Taking into Account Users' Views, Online Context and Algorithmic Estimation." *Sociology* 51(6), 1149–1168.

Wilson, D. R., and T. R. Martinez (2003). "The General Inefficiency of Batch Training for Gradient Descent Learning." *Neural Networks* 16(10), 1429–1451. http://dx.doi.org/10.1016/S0893-6080(03)00138-2.

Won, D., Z. C. Steinert-Threlkeld, and J. Joo (2017). "Protest Activity Detection and Perceived Violence Estimation from Social Media Images." In: *Proceedings of the 25th ACM International Conference on Multimedia.* http://arxiv.org/abs/1709.06204.

You, Q. et al. (2015). "Robust Image Sentiment Analysis using Progressively Trained and Domain Transferred Deep Networks." In: *The Twenty-Ninth AAAI Conference*, pp. 381–388.

Zhang, H., and J. Pan (2019). "CASM: A Deep Learning Approach for Identifying Collective Action Events with Text and Image Data from Social Media." *Sociological Methodology* 49(1), 1–57.

Zhang, Q., and S.-C. Zhu (2018). "Visual Interpretability for Deep Learning: a Survey." http://arxiv.org/abs/1802.00614.

Zhao, J., et al. (2017). "Men Also Like Shopping: Reducing Gender Bias Amplification using Corpus-Level Constraints." *CoRR* abs/1707.0. http://arxiv.org/abs/1707.09457.

Zhu, X., and D. Ramanan (2012). "Face Detection, Pose Estimation, and Landmark Estimation in the Wild." In: *International Conf. on Computer Vision and Pattern Recognition (CVPR)*, pp. 2879–2886.

Cambridge Elements ☰

Quantitative and Computational Methods for the Social Sciences

R. Michael Alvarez

California Institute of Technology

R. Michael Alvarez has taught at the California Institute of Technology his entire career, focusing on elections, voting behavior, election technology, and research methodologies. He has written or edited a number of books (recently, *Computational Social Science: Discovery and Prediction, and Evaluating Elections: A Handbook of Methods and Standards*) and numerous academic articles and reports.

Nathaniel Beck

New York University

Nathaniel Beck is Professor of Politics at NYU (and Affiliated Faculty at the NYU Center for Data Science) where he has been since 2003; before which he was Professor of Political Science at the University of California, San Diego. He is the founding editor of the quarterly, *Political Analysis*. He is a fellow of both the American Academy of Arts and Sciences and the Society for Political Methodology.

About the Series

The Elements Series *Quantitative and Computational Methods for the Social Sciences* contains short introductions and hands-on tutorials to innovative methodologies. These are often so new that they have no textbook treatment or no detailed treatment on how the method is used in practice. Among emerging areas of interest for social scientists, the series presents machine learning methods, the use of new technologies for the collection of data and new techniques for assessing causality with experimental and quasi-experimental data.

Cambridge Elements ☰

Quantitative and Computational Methods for the Social Sciences